A TEMPORARY STRANGER

OTHER BOOKS BY JAMIE REID

Poetry
The Man Whose Path Was on Fire
Prez: Homage to Lester Young
Mad Boys
I. Another. The Space Between: Selected Poems

Biography
Diana Krall: The Language of Love
Chris Isaak: Wicked Games

A Temporary Stranger

Homages, Poems, Recollections

by
Jamie Reid

ANVIL PRESS | 2017

Copyright © 2017 by the estate of Jamie Reid

All rights reserved. No part of this book may be reproduced by any means without the prior written permission of the publisher, with the exception of brief passages in reviews. Any request for photocopying or other reprographic copying of any part of this book must be directed in writing to ACCESS: The Canadian Copyright Licensing Agency, One Yonge Street, Suite 800, Toronto, Ontario, Canada, M5E 1E5.

Anvil Press Publishers Inc.
P.O. Box 3008, Main Post Office
Vancouver, B.C. V6B 3X5 Canada
www.anvilpress.com

Library and Archives Canada Cataloguing in Publication

Reid, Jamie, 1941-2015, author
    A temporary stranger / Jamie Reid. -- 1st edition.

Poems.
ISBN 978-1-77214-098-9 (softcover)

    I. Title.

PS8585.E6012T46 2017   C811'.54   C2017-901251-7

Printed and bound in Canada
Edited by Karl Siegler
Cover design by Derek von Essen
Cover photo by Gabor Gasztonyi
Interior by HeimatHouse
Represented in Canada by Publishers Group Canada
Distributed by Raincoast Books

The publisher gratefully acknowledges the financial assistance of the Canada Council for the Arts, the Canada Book Fund, and the Province of British Columbia through the B.C. Arts Council and the Book Publishing Tax Credit.

This book is dedicated in Jamie's name
to the community of writers and artists of Vancouver
whom he nourished and who nourished him in return.

Contents

- *9* Foreword
- *13* Homages
- *35* Fake Poems
- *63* Recollections

Foreword
Karl Siegler

On the morning of the day Jamie "returned to the spirit world" as his friend Leonard George so eloquently put it, he had saved the manuscript of this three-part book into the drafts folder of his e-mail program, poised to be sent to Anvil Press for publication—to become a treasure for us to enjoy in the midst of our lives.

At its centre is his masterwork, 'Fake Poems,' which he had begun to write some time before May of 2012. Why did he call them Fake Poems? In part, he says in his introduction to them, because "There is no art on earth that can fully represent the exact and flowing experience of viewing stone within the flow of water and the waving light within the water and around the stone, and the subsequent sense of awe and beauty that arises in the interaction between the seer and the seen.... In that sense, all art is fake..."

He had also stated in a May, 2012 interview with Vancouver Co-op Radio's *Wax Poetic*, "I feel that they leave too much unsaid.... And the problem is it's very hard to separate the fake from the genuine.... I haven't completed [them] yet and the method is still being resolved and in the process I named one a fake poem but it turned out to be genuine, and now I have to rename it." So, clearly for Jamie, fake poems can and do coexist with genuine poems. What then, is the difference?

The complete sequence of his twenty-one 'Fake Poems' is presented here along with Jamie's 'explanation' of them by way of an introduction ("There is reality, and there is art..."); and, as he intended, they are bracketed by both a genuine prelude poem, 'Warbler,' and a genuine coda poem, 'Where to Find Grace'; along with his final footnote on the series as well.

In order to contextualize the transcendent and liberating departure which these new poems represent in Jamie Reid's life and work, this book begins with his 'Homages,' previously published in an earlier version by Pooka Press in 2009, and concludes with his 'Recollections,' published on various occasions along the way.

Of course, any attempt to distinguish between genuine and fake poems leads one unavoidably to questions of literary theory or poetics, as it did for Jamie throughout his life. And where better to begin to answer those questions than at the beginning:

After announcing his subject, "Poetry in itself and of its various kinds," Aristotle opens the first book of literary criticism ever written in the western tradition, published circa 330 BCE, with the statement: "Epic poetry and Tragedy, Comedy also and Dithyrambic [lyric] poetry, and the music of the flute and of the lyre in most of their forms, are all in their general conception modes of imitation." He continues for the rest of his short treatise to be as clear as possible about what poetry imitates, and in all cases in his *Poetics* that turns out to be an action as we experience it in nature. Art, for Aristotle, imitates life as it is actively and publicly lived in its particulars, and poetry is therefore itself an action.

This is the exact opposite of what Wordsworth claims poetry to be in the preface to his *Lyrical Ballads* published over two millennia later: "Poetry is the spontaneous overflow of powerful feelings: it takes its origin from emotion recollected in tranquility." Art, for Wordsworth, exists outside of life as it is passively and privately recollected after the fact, and poetry is therefore itself a product of reification, an object — a profit taken from an exploitation of nature — a surplus.

These two diametrically opposed views of poetics mark the parameters of Jamie Reid's life-long preoccupation with the place of poetry in his life. There can be no question on which side of this dialectic Jamie found himself as he set out on his journey through the world, nor on which side of it he planted his oar when he arrived at the threshing floor of that journey's end: Aristotle's.

There is also no doubt that during the middle of his life Jamie experienced, not a crisis of faith (because on all questions of doing versus believing he remained steadfastly on the side of good works), but a loss of direction which, like Dante's before him, would require the presence of guides for him to rediscover what bpNichol had called "the one path, the true path."

In the first section of this collection, 'Homages,' Jamie introduces us to those guides, and says of their poems: "These texts therefore might as well have been as ancient as the Rosetta Stone, because the poems I fashioned from them are really more like translations of translations than fully original works…."

In this book's third section, 'Recollections,' we encounter memory—not as a form of nostalgia for a bygone golden age of a romanticised pastoral arcadia viewed from the privileged position of leisure afforded our poets by the accumulated intellectual capital of the industrial and technological revolutions since the 18th century, but as an historical record of who did what when, and to what end, throughout the counterculture revolution that shaped the lives of Jamie Reid and his companions over the past six decades. Here, in these stories that read like transcriptions from an oral tradition, Jamie's lucid gaze does not waver from the discipline of historical materialism that informed all of his actions with an objectivity to which we have grown unaccustomed in our time of identity politics and the selfie. Quite astonishingly, he accomplishes in them something that no historian could possibly duplicate: a credible presentation of the simple authenticity of having been there. As he says in "The Legacy of Warren Tallman," "…it is important for all of us to remember the past, to create history, and to recreate history, to take from memory, recorded or otherwise, what the present requires, so I am bound to do the same."

It is in the central section of this book, in the 'Fake Poems,' where Jamie realizes that in the making of poetry, like that of history, we are bound to create not a reproduction of the past, which has become lost to us forever, but simply what the present requires—a reenactment of the past, because: "Any poem is an impossibility of language that does not end, a remain, a survivor, something that has appeared. It is always unfinished, unconcluded, and free."

HOMAGES

HOMAGES

Introduction: Reinventing Voices

The procedures I followed in making these poems were different entirely from the practice of spirit mediums, through whom the dead are said to speak from another existence. In these poems, it turns out I tried to do the opposite, seeking allowance to speak through the invented voices of the ghosts of dead authors who mostly wrote in French. In a way, they are a kind of monologue with these authors, but also, I hope, an introduction to a dialogue, silent or otherwise, with readers of these poems.

I relied on texts the living authors wrote, which I read in interlinear translation. These texts therefore might as well have been as ancient as the Rosetta Stone, because the poems I fashioned from them are really more like translations of translations than fully original works, shamelessly borrowing and copying themes, motifs, ideas and styles from their models.

Some parts went missing in the transmission: Francois Villon, who is not celebrated in a poem of his own, seemed to me a ghost beyond and behind all the other ghosts. Some others that might have been included if I had discovered how to do so, but didn't: Le Comte de Lautréamont, Stéphane Mallarme, Antonin Artaud.

I have tried throughout the process to situate the poems within my own real garden, among my own circle of friends, among the normal run of days and tasks, among familiar things and matters, the deeds and thoughts of my own daily life.

The invention of these ghosts has allowed me the superb freedom of speaking in several voices not quite my own, more open to the uncertainty of ephemeral suggestion, to the "other" and the transmigrational "beyond" that art and poetry can sometimes reach toward.

—Jamie Reid, January 2009

homage to jack spicer

I'm weary of this dialogue with the dead.
They talk too much, but they don't listen.
Their ears are stuffed with dirt, or worse,
burned away in calcium fires.

Why are we haunted by these particular ghosts?
They dream in triplicate: once for themselves,
once for us, and once again for the world at large.

They whisper rather than speaking.
They are gathered unceremoniously
at the bottom of the garden,
puffing Gauloises, cussing
under their breath.

What did we do to deserve this?
The silence is better and more meaningful.

What happened to the notion of harps in the afterlife,
the music of the spheres,
which the dead were supposed to hear
better than we do?

My friend, a Doukhobor, once transcribed
the voice of the ghost of Federico,
never having read his books.

It came to him out of the bottom of a wine glass
while he was eating pumpkin seeds.

Peter spoke Spanish perfectly, though with a Mexican accent,
but Federico spoke to him in English, anyway.
Maybe it was Peter Sorokin, sneaking around

in the afterlife, putting on masks and disguises,
begging him to go away with him to fascist Uruguay
and stay well clear of communist Cuba.

This poem shouldn't end this way,
But sadly it does. The dead
know less than we do.

homage to charles baudelaire

The fog of Paris encloses you, your hard sharp nose,
recessive chest, whining words from the shadows,
voice like a wheedling cat, someone once said,
his name now almost forgotten,
unlike yours.

You have eyed them all. Within your incised soul,
you've dug in all their sicknesses forever. The fog
seeps in beneath your upper eyelids,
a slight and pleasant sting brings cold tears,
as onions do, pain without significant remorse.

Your white handkerchief
strokes them from your cheek
impatiently.

Nature's living temple is defiled
as you knowingly observe,
deliberately indifferent.

Strolling alone in the darkened park,
feeling the caresses of the eyes of the trees,
their familiar glances
of forever disappointed love.

homage to arthur rimbaud

"La musique savante manque á notre désir." (Arthur Rimbaud)

Let's say there's this knowing music everywhere,
filling all the air,
even when unwanted. Let's say
there's never been enough silence,
though so much desired
everywhere.

Let's say a blue and perfect silence at last arrives,
like the silence that fell upon you in Africa at last.

Will not that silence, like the music,
also always fail
to satisfy our full desire?

Unloveable Arthur…

homage to andre breton

It would look like an abandoned pair of shoes on the waterfront,
like somebody else's puddle on the sidewalk,
like the view from a small bridge across a small creek
forded by baptismal acolytes like sleepwalkers.
Among them, a tourist, a would-be Jesus,
shaking his long locks, dozy Dionysius,
large head of hair on a massive head.

It would be like a moment of waking in which the trees outside
are momentarily confused in consciousness
with the design on the curtains inside the room.

It would be forbidden in this new society
to make the distinction between sleeping and waking.

The Registry of Dreams and Nightmares
would have priority over every other ministry,
open only at night, attended by
the half-awake, the half-blind, the half-deaf,
the incompletely known.

New rules issued every morning
countermanded every night.

The trains would depart today, arriving yesterday.
Obviously nothing would ever be on time. In fact,
it would be against the law to be on time.
Later rewarded. Earlier punished.

Advertisements begin with the words
"Be sure to stay away from all of this."
The food arrives at the table long before the diners,
cleared off the tables before anyone can touch it,
surrounded with whispers of poison.

Each day's work begins
with the analysis
of the previous night's dreams.

homage to apollinaire 1

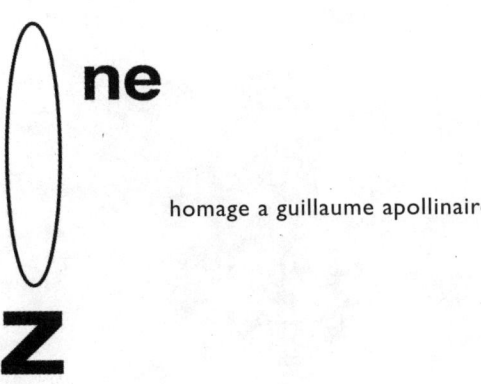

homage a guillaume apollinaire

homage to apollinaire 2

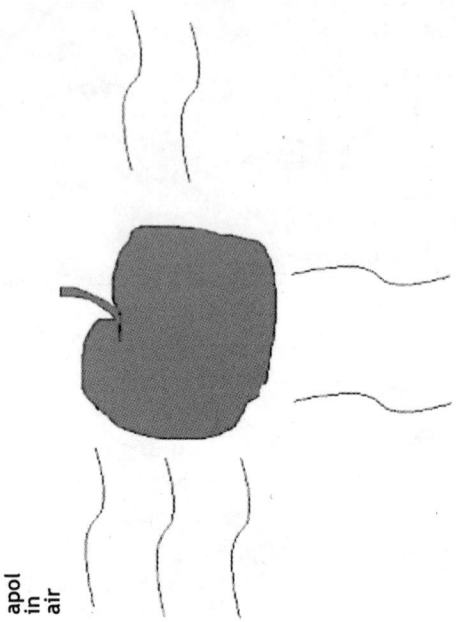

homage to saint-john perse

A yes there were winds and the seas arose in the midst of their action
molecules of air, molecules of water, whipped up
under the clouds, the whistling, the sound of such an immense rush,
the shuffle of feet in cities visited by sand in the midst of those same winds,
the smell of distance, of spices, of gold, of the excrement of heretofore
unknown animals, nourished by unknown vegetables.

Caught as though in these gusts, gusts in their hearts, men and women
driven into motion, wandered hither and thither, peering here and there,
as if a vast voice had called them and drawn them, to go and to come,
to disperse and to gather, to depart, sometimes forever,
only rarely to return as a visitor, half or more of a stranger
to the source of the winds that pulled them or drove them away.

How to come home again
when all that the wind brings says stay where you are, where
even if it is bad, it is better than the here and the now that you left behind.

The whistling is the sound of the dead, no longer of any use to us,
those who have already done all that they could and gone over.
The wind tears us away from them,
knowing our own needs better than we know them ourselves,
to begin again, again to begin.

O listen to the winds, they tell of the past and drive the sails
that lead to the unpredictable, unforgettable future.

homage to max jacob

I was severely mistaken in writing to a poet acquaintance that Max Jacob took his own life.

In fact, it was only and maybe merely his afterlife he took, and he took it deliberately as a Catholic, which he had become by choice, not birth.

After converting to the Church of Rome, he joined the gang of poets and artists on Montmartre in order to sin disgracefully, so he said.

It was not for this reason that the Gestapo later arrested him and put him in the concentration camp where he died of lung disease. It was because he had been born a Jew.

His conversion therefore completely failed to save his life.

I hope my poet acquaintance, who told me that he feels his own work is most like Max Jacob's, does not come to suffer a similar fate.

May he contrive to enjoy all sins untrammelled, no matter how considerable, without feeling any need for punishment, as did poor Catholic Max.

May I, too, live in hope
to do the same, dear,
merciful God.

homage to pierre reverdy

after a while they stopped their talking
a turn to the right
heel and toe
walking on together in the night

how simply the darkness slipped its noose
the news came over the wire
ending their silence
soon enough their footsteps also ceased

they came to the station
the doors were all found closed
the windows showed nothing inside

the last arrivals had already departed for the centre of the city
no one new was expected
on that exact particular night
the trains arranged silently in the yard
the sound of waiting unfinished
a jet plane left behind a silent trail in the sky

a billion billion alphabet footmarks
appeared upon
the internet
to mark the day of my friend's birth.

homage to paul eluard

the birds of the lawn what
do they have to do
with poetry what
do their wings say
about words and things
or words
about wings

even if they catch the rays of the sunset
flashing, even if
each bird sings

they have already gone lightly
to their home in the night, heads
tucked under their wings, song
unsung…
words unspoken
under the tongue.

Meanwhile
poetry burrows, burrows,
borrowing the colours of the earth,
paying no interest. Gone
in the flutter of an eyelid
the flutter of a wing,
the fluttering flattering tongues.

homage to jacques prevert

first you name a thing, a cup of coffee, say,
and then some cream to add to it, a bit of sugar,
a spoon to stir it with. Whisper
the name of lips.

Someone drinks, eats, then goes out of doors.

The poet rests his head in his hands,
quite happily.

This is called the making of poems.
More like a list of names and deeds.

Some years ago, on this very day,
my friend was born.

Paroles. Histoires.

homage to francis ponge

I want to be clean again, so
bring me some soap, bring me
the slime of a snail, a match
for this cigarette, a moment only
to create ashes
for the soil of my garden,

the space in which to make one single
indecipherable
footprint,
a finger with which to trace
a single letter not even a word
on the glass of the window,
the soft evanescent bubbles of the soap
to wipe the window clean,
to mark the day and the moment
of my friend's birth.

homage to francis picabia

always the flatulent dadaist playboy
with your fancy sports cars emitting
various powders decorating the nose
surrounded always with
the not quite delicate odour of obscenity
effluvium of feathered armpits
deliberate but not entirely impenetrable
semi-oracular feverish obscurity
never smelled a hot dog
to embellish the otherwise perfect
nasal obsession
plastered with parrot feathers, crow feathers
feet fresh blistered from the heat of the beach
a gustatory mendicant
the grim simian grin
murderous repartee
with the sunshine
leaving behind the odour
of petroleum farts
well-tuned engines
and other sarcastic exactulations
what a scream

homage to tristan tzara

In the gravel courtyard
of your semi-famous former mansion,
in Montmartre,
today musicians play
some amplified flamenco,
& well-dressed drinkers play at bowls,
black balls tossed high into the air.

In the grassy lane
adjacent to this stone-walled courtyard,
the strolling tourist
comes upon a dark and leafy bower
overgrown with branches.

Within this darkened grove,
there sits immovably
a lump of indiscernible matter,
almost as tall as a man,
as wide and as thick
as a man is tall.

At first glance, and even afterwards
neither eyes nor fingers can easily discern
if this pocked and pitted presence
is animal, vegetable or mineral,
a meteorite fallen from the sky,
a 12 ton bit of worthless metal slag,
or something entirely hybrid,
entirely in-between
the natural and the made.

There it sits, disconsolate,
hidden, isolate,
covered with droppings
from the branches, dust,
bits of dried leaves,
desiccated fronds,
the webs of touring insects.

Some steps beyond the copse,
in the distance
against the pale silvery evening sky
the Eiffel Tower upraised
like the solitary finger
of a giant iron skeleton
somewhere beneath the earth of Paris.

A moment of silent freedom comes upon me,
completely inarticulate.

Approximate man. Approximate monster.

FAKE POEMS

FAKE POEMS

There is reality and there is art, and art is part of reality and part of nature which is itself artless and goes on without concern for anyone's aesthetic sense or scientific sense or any other kind of human sense. In that sense, nature is innocent and indifferent, the very opposite of art, which is most often artful and contentious. Art and discourse dream of richly sampling all the riches present here on earth long before human beings arrived with all their art and artifice.

Take any stone in any stream, available to any human vision. There is no art on earth that can fully represent the exact and flowing experience of viewing stone within the flow of water and the waving light within the water and around the stone, and the subsequent sense of awe and beauty that arises in the interaction between the seer and the seen.

In that sense, all art is fake, because the artificial means we use to represent those living objects cannot duplicate the quality of human sensual experience, in which sensation and intellect run inseparably together. Art and artificiality for that reason are entirely inseparable. All art, in that sense, must be, in some sense, false.

As a boy I learned, though badly, a way to move while trying to move the ball or puck past defenders on the other side in the game. The head goes one way, the body another, the ball or puck slips by unhindered, the movement called a fake. These poems, at their best, shake and lean the head in one direction in order to move the body's stem in the opposite direction. All of them are rooted in language and its easiest vagaries, which always speak for themselves, even as I intervene with them.

WARBLER

how language at least English
deteriorates no longer says
what it used to say sentences no longer
than they used to be but without
periods no thought ever completed run on
into the next one too much expected reality
overcrowded too few words one word doing
multiple duty what was actually
meant the mouth the page
cannot contain ambiguity
burgeons less for distraction
more than attraction all's
garbled that warbler warbles distinctively
in the very far distance

FAKE POEM 1

The last day was easy I needed to talk I needed to talk it slipped out of me like an animal out of its burrow and whipped around the tree whistling under its breath and breaking the air unseasonably with a quick turn of phrase as quick as the broken wind as it fell from the trees moaning quietly as if interrupted in its sleep uncomprehending the silence of that insane evening whenever we spoke it was as if as if went backwards from the air to the mouth from the ear to the air until that last breathless moment when at last I fell quiet, swallowing tenaciously

FAKE POEM 2

Go get it the lady said
it's right over there
under the tree
can't you see

well wait then
it will almost surely
reappear because
it never wished
to disappear in the first place
and knows very well it has to come back
sometime, whether we believe it or not

it can't be lying
because it has no way
of knowing the truth
about itself
with any certainty

It is important
to get used to that
because it too
needs to get used to it
however badly
and however ill-informed
no way around it

FAKE POEM 3

Let's face it she always used to say that's not the way it's going to be you aren't what you think you are and you'll never learn to sing like frank you're a sensitive boy and I'm very proud of you but I hope you never lose yourself in false ambition and turn against your mother who loves you almost as much as anything almost as much as these words she's speaking now as if she would never shut up let's face it and she doesn't thankfully the last one that truly cared let's face it

FAKE POEM 4

Yesterday I thought that way until I went to bed my regulated waking thinking interrupted in my dream the shadow of a man walked through the very transparent window through which I viewed my world disrupted what I had been pleased to call my chain of thought turned out to be not a hard discrete chain at all but a smooth continuous though not entirely seamless skein and thereafter a colourless stream and thereafter again an interrupted stream broke in splashes on the pavement slipped away dwindling in a rush of colours never to be redeemed again but never mind a new skin replaced the old in time and the same two feet stood again as always too squarely on the ground as always walking up the stairs and down again and up

FAKE POEM 5

for Vic Toews & Stephen Harper

Writing fake poems is hard
to remain believable
harder still
this illusion in which they persist,
recreating that they know better
than the rest of us
against all those others
who also pretend to know better
but differently
and too they too must remain
so fiercely staunch
in spite of all misgivings
that those others also do not show
how amazing the government
believes it can lecture others
on our behalf
we should lecture back
as best we can
they do not answer questions
but persist in spite of it
delivering consistent falsehoods
with proud consistency
never flagging in their senseless waving

FAKE POEM 6

Going over old poetry like washing hands, a habit of the conscious pilot navigating by instrument, blind in the fog remembrance is, the wish to find that perfect moment finding something else entirely instead, a wakening from that old furred sleep, I'd dream again somehow we'll get there secretly no one watching now no one caring less or more the disappearance into the past and into the future too one passes oneself in the fog again unseen forgotten

FAKE POEM 7

Mulling various philosophical concepts the relation between being and thought and thinking and saying and drinking and dying he dived for the muffle of consciousness curiously under the welt of the darkening sky wishfully wistful the rope of belonging and safety knotted extravagantly around the waist of his life much already having passed under the bridge along with the long gone canoes and snowshoes on the bank of the river in several cities the buildings looked out at him blankly blinking their indifferent lights left out in the cold

FAKE POEM 8

humanitarian concerns again initiate new rounds of voting and bombing the guilty the concerned the innocent the activist embroiled men with guns scurrying amidst the fires explosions yells prayers moans other men with guns are gathering and waiting in the wings a wider conflict imminent the protection of the innocent here and elsewhere everywhere pictures of barbecued children to prove necessity of intervention cures worse than the disease lies all around the truth somewhere in between but still in black and white don't forget the red of blood burned flesh served up as today's best news and technicolor television demanding belief those not on their side on the side of monsters until the truth comes out at last much later much too late to provide relief the harm never again undone anglo america the source and centre of all things holy and humane orders up new fires far from the safe home fires to save us all all cheer and then look serious please then smile everything turn out all right stop worrying

FAKE POEM 9
(on a Hannah Hoch photomontage)

The body is female
the head male
a human demon figure
emerges from a box-like skirt form
black at the top
spread out
like a squared off skirt
below her
intersected by two broad contrasting stripes
no feet appear beneath the skirt
one hand pressed to the waist
disappears into
the top of the box-like skirt
the other arm
venus de milo style
goes missing
the torso
seems to be tattooed
the nippled breasts
which establish the figure
as female appear as
part of a white half-sweater
that covers the tattooed body
from rib-cage to neck
above which the mask
of the face in polished black
from each side of its long nose
two broad white tusks are growing downward

FAKE POEM 10

You were not born alone,
& you will not die alone.
Someone will be there with you always,
even in that echoing room,
even when you don't prefer it.

Without them you cannot be born, die,
or remain alive even into the next moment.

As soon as you have come to speech,
you will never speak yourself alone,
but always all those others, too,
long dead ancestors, ancient mothers,
your nearby contemporaries, those outside,
those inside,
still waiting to be born,
the multitudes of people who have never known you
and whom you've never known.

You are their very own ghost,
their uninvited guest,
their unmentionable sister.

They are your guides. Always present,
there is never any need to call them.
Without them you will surely become
permanently, irretrievably lost.

In the meantime,
try to remember, then try to forget.
The memory will neither fully arrive, nor fully go away.

Soon enough you will go missing forever.
There are so many who will never guess
where you have gone.

FAKE POEM 11

The way that consciousness and speech are prone to drift
when prone and lying lifelike laying down the letter of the
law where speech is strict and ordered no thread lost or stray
we go away from ourselves lose ourselves in mental play the
play of words light on leaves an inner moving picture a dream
one image to the next bubbles and waves arising shadows
and reflections hidden in the stream the odd bright fish
flickering in the shallows shows its colors

FAKE POEM 12

Throwing words together as though into a box of toys. It cannot be done without the existence of the words like the toys in advance already. The language and its words invade your most private bedroom. They kiss in the bathroom when you're alone. You talk to yourself as to an imagined other who persistently fails to imagine you in return. The mirror returns the image of a temporary stranger who soon enough comes to fit inside a newly minted slightly glowing image. This poem is like a set of dentures that does not quite fit inside the mouth, these words that leak out as I speak. Whose voice do you actually mean?

FAKE POEM 13

The basic idea is to create the appearance of a spontaneous anti-poem, fake because it is not entirely spontaneous or automatic, nor fully deliberate either. The deliberate may be changed to appear accidental, the accidental deliberately altered. It is important that there should be the appearance of mistaken words and phrases. Nothing else will suffice to disguise the confusion between the I's and the o you's, between looking and seeing, thinking and knowing. Artifice either obvious, or hidden with great care. The appearance of innocence and carelessness, but only the appearance. All resolution apparent only. Pleasure appears alongside dis-ease.

FAKE POEM 14

Seen through the lens of a camera, they seemed to move
through various planes of glass.
In another world, they found trouble
making out their heads from their asses.

The garment of want, unspeakable itself.
Spoken through them, the speakable surrogate
Of the poverty-stricken, the experts
Who came to save them and speak in their name.

A permanent fog seemed to flow from their words,
Impossible to find the world there,
No earth, no water, no animals, no birds,
Nothing but language,
the hum and the effluvium of the cheating word.

FAKE POEM 15

How easily this music
enters the ear
and thence the brain, erasing
one channel
another opens.

As seawater rocks
into the cracks
in the rocks
in the night.

The air opens because
the mind contains and occupies
no space.

No opening no enclosure,
only emptiness
fully engorged.

Like the air, its smoke and its dew,
the music enters my ears,
resides inside
silently
ringing

FAKE POEM 16

The way
      the mind
moves and works in its own silence,
 slipping
      so quietly from one
thought to the next,
as things float on water,
no seam between.

Never know it's there
until its reappears,
that not quite fullness of the half idea,
the low tide of the moon and mind
passive receptor to itself.

Absence of action or gesture,
around a word or an image,
lips form the whisper,
the singular aura of singular feeling

all those secret
cracks & creakings
underneath
underneath.

FAKE POEM 17

The trees,
though we take them
for granted, remain
large & marvellous,

always
in motion,
whispering.

They wait, but they wait
for no one and for nothing in particular.

They hear the sound of the birds
as they fall
from the sky
to the shoulders of their branches.

Hear this,
the trees are saying,
hear this.

FAKE POEM 18
WHAT LIFE HOLDS (for Pierre Coupey on his 70th birthday)

What falls from the sky & the trees
what weeps upward from under,
from inside outside, from outside in,
marks, scars, bruises, stains, signs, smears, blots, clots, accumulations
of oil & moisture, charcoal blurs from extinguished fires,
the bones of the feet of a poet
that cross(ed) a mottled field,
& was killed in his tracks
tracks &
   trajectories,
an alphabet,
a set of newly-invented hieroglyphics,
squiggles on the earth from a stick,
musical notes, words on a line or staff,
hands held up, holding up
the hidden,
what's brought in and left behind with the tide,
dropped leaves and branches

the signs
     vital signs
signs of life & passage

II

A living space marked by a half-hidden cross,
the grid erased or originally undrawn
from top to bottom, bottom to top,
each hard edge to each soft middle,
a space that opens,

a mouth that speaks.

III (method map, erased commentary)

imagine	language	paint	work	
subtext	many	voices	combined	abstract
writing	before &	after	writing	
overgrown	vegetation	tombstones	overturned	meditative
colour	shape	paintings	reflect	
genesis	poetry &	literary		allusions

FAKE POEM 19

dear jack trying
to write the poems i don't know
how to write how to say
what up to now
remains unsaid
speaking of the dead &
to the dead i miss you
all so much as much
as all those living friends old lovers
unreachable all the kisses missed
the jests the mists of feeling

FAKE POEM 20

The horror of
the news today, the smell
of death, reported body parts,
lost memories,
neither victim nor perpetrator
fully present, witnesses
suborned or subslain,
the truth beyond
the deliberate veils of the words
unconscionable

FAKE POEM 21

think I am going to be copying this latest style. Someone bound to be listening, even at the very last edge of everything. Turning the corner without much hope. Grace and faith long gone. This newest style seems to say just so. It's about being bereft, about tearing one's hair, about not knowing the way out, somehow coming to like it and boldly saying so. One wan smile, the carpet of hair on the floor, the locked door, insistent beating of the rap.

WHERE TO FIND GRACE

Under the kitchen table with the flour
and the cat dish, in the kitchen sink
with the supper dishes and the bubbles of soap.

Behind half-closed eyelids in the sunlight.

Round About Midnight
in the moonlit garden.

Two steps down into
the Qu'Appelle Valley in April sunshine.

Called by one's own name in the street,
an unfamiliar voice on any uncertain gray day.

Where women are talking and laughing,
watching their children at play.

The water that falls from the sky
always a grace.

Equally a grace, evaporation in sunlight.

The very same water always
falling again somewhere else
taken up again, and again condensing and falling,
& again taken up.

Only to know about this and to be able
to think about it.
Impossible grace.

Inescapably surrounded.
Like the rain of any ordinary day.

Fake poem note:

"…in my opinion no work is finished. I think, rather, that totality does not exist, is not possible, and is not desirable. What exists are fragments, remains, ruins that do not admit to a totality. Any poem is an impossibility of language that does not end, a remain, a survivor, something that has appeared. It is always unfinshed, unconcluded, and free."
—Chus Pato
43rd Poetry International Festival Rotterdam,
May 31, 2012

RECOLLECTIONS

CURT LANG

The uprising sponsored by the beat generation sort of began in 1955 with the obscenity trial of Allen Ginsberg's *Howl*, but it had only begun to reach the outport colonial fringe in Vancouver in 1958 with the opening of the first of a series of what the mainstream Vancouver population would call beatnik joints. The first of these was the Black Spot, a jazz club in the residential Dunbar district, frequented mostly by university students. The next place that opened was The Den, on Harwood Street just west of Burrard.

It was there while I was still in my last year of high school (in fact, in Grade XIII) that I first saw Curt Lang. My mother had warned me in worried tones that she had heard that the Little Heidelberg, another place on the circuit of the nascent Vancouver bohemian community, was nothing less than a nest of neo-nazis. My own later investigations showed that it really was a nest of near reds and anarchists — the politics of everybody I ever met in the Howe Street version of the Little Heidelberg and its later reincarnation on Robson Street was decidedly oriented toward the ideological left. Curt was part of the crowd that circled around these enticingly mysterious places. I knew Curt and Curt's name before he knew me. At first, I thought he might be one of the neo-nazis with his Germanic sounding name and his close-cropped hair, his rangy athlete's physique, his prideful upright posture, and an overwhelmingly confident demeanour that verged on arrogance. Once I eavesdropped on a conversation he was having with the tall and wistful blonde woman who sometimes sang jazz songs at The Den. He was talking about the possibility of a political crisis in Canada, and to the sceptical, somewhat goggle-eyed silence of the canary, as we called her, told her that if there ever were such a crisis "we would all be incarcerated." It was the first time I had ever heard the word, although I had come across it in my reading without knowing what it meant. Its harsh vowels and its mixture of plosive and hissing consonants, made me feel that the word designated activity somewhere between being burned alive and being wrapped in barbed wire. It had never occurred to me before that moment anyone might think that people could be sent to prison in Canada for their political beliefs and activities. In this sense, it was a major step toward a self-awakening that actually came much later. So, in at least that sense, Curt first appeared to me as a person who was very much ahead of his time, even though I have since learned that his social and political understandings were rooted in the working class culture of the 1940s and 1950s, with its broad internationalism and its interest in all the intellectual currents of the time. The bookstores in Vancouver were minor centres of that culture back then. Binky Marx, a legendary bookseller, held a kind of court in the paperback basement of Duthie Books on Robson, and just across the street was the bookstore of Doug and Hannah Kaye where Curt sometimes hung around drinking wine and holding deep conversation in the back with the proprietors and their friend Al Purdy, one of Canada's most famous and beloved poets, though little known in those days.

Although I knew who he was, and although the circles that I travelled in sometimes intersected with Curt's circles — I must have exchanged words and nods with him at parties that we attended jointly — I don't remember any significant conversation I had with him until 1963, when we lived in the same block of decaying old west-end houses on the last two blocks of West Pender Street, an enclave of Vancouver's new but burgeoning bohemia. In a basement club on that same street we found ourselves together at a poetry reading, and because above all else, Curt loved to talk and there was no one else there that night with whom he could indulge his love of loquacity, he spoke to me at length for the first time. He praised the poem read by Grady Moore and then made some critical comments about my own reading. He remarked on the intensity of my poems and critically added that I was trying to bring it out of an awfully fucking tight key hole, as he put it, and he wondered if I had a Roman Catholic upbringing on that account. The combination of confidentiality and provocation in his approach appealed to me, and I thought he had given voice to a real insight. Far from being upset by his criticism, I was flattered by the intelligent attention, and therefore took his comments seriously ever afterward and tried to loosen up my approach to language and expression.

There were two centres of new poetic activity in the city in earliest part of those days: one was at the University of British Columbia, centred around Warren Tallman and the group known as the TISH poets, of which I was one. The other was loosely centred around the Vancouver School of Art, and Jack Shadbolt might be considered its very distant sponsor—later, that group was to centre around bill bissett and his blewointment press on Fourth Avenue. Warren Tallman referred to this second centre as the "downtown poets," though the designation was very loose. Curt belonged to that group of artists and poets which included himself, Roy Kiyooka, Al Neil, Fred Douglas, Jock Hearn, Judith Copithorne, Maxine Gadd, and the partners of these artists who appeared at parties, usually dressed in black and with heavily mascaraed eyes. bill bissett was also a sometime member of this group.

That second group drank together, talked together, engaged in projects of one kind or another and stood in proud opposition to everything else that was going on. Their characteristic attitude was provocative irreverence toward the institutions of the society and the prevailing ideologies. To speak the truth about the situation now, these art school and downtown types knew more about the sources and direction of modernism than the university-educated poets. Apart from that, their understanding was more closely connected to the ins and outs of real life and real artistic production and toward production in general. Curt, for example, may have wanted to be an artist, but he was forced to make his living in those days as a skilled tradesman, a welder. In a certain way, he was as much at odds with his own situation and contradictions as he was with the society at large. Curt was a total and unrelenting intellectual rebel. As such, he was at war with what was, and there was no generally held idea, notion, or practice that escaped his critical and often satirical attention.

In the years following, I came to know Curt better through meeting him at the Alcazar, where the artists congregated and talked during those times, and at the home on Arbutus in Kitsilano that he shared with my friend Peter Auxier in the middle 1960s. Curt was marginally involved in a variety of artistic and literary enterprises, and characteristically, he was critically at odds with what others were doing. He was publishing some poetry in bill bissett's *blewointment* magazine, and he was working on a small painting. The first instance of fence art in Vancouver had been completed that summer, organized by the local artist Frank Lewis. Curt professed to be appalled at the poor quality of the fence art while applauding the idea of fence art in general. Through those months, he worked meticulously on his small canvas, a picture of a house on a hillside at night, insisting that his own painting was an exemplar of the kind of care that was required to produce genuine fence art that would properly reflect the community's feelings and sense of history and belonging. His main project at that time was the building of his first fibre-glass canoe, which proceeded continuously in the basement through one stage after another, as Curt struggled with each of the technical problems of building the frame for the mold, mixing the fibre-glass, etc. His aim was to accomplish the building of a canoe made with his own design and built with his own original methods. The final result was a convincingly elegant looking canoe with one pointed end and one square end. The canoe actually floated and could be paddled through the water off Kitsilano Beach and was in every respect completely seaworthy except for its very alarming behaviour on the water. The fibre-glass walls of the canoe were so thin that the entire craft wiggled and wobbled alarmingly from end to end in the water like a snake, which did not inspire much of a sense of confidence in its apparent seaworthiness.

The usual remark made against Curt at that time was that he talked too much, criticised too much and actually did too little in the way of art and actual performance, but Curt was indifferent to this complaint. He often said that if he had a choice in life about what he might do forever, he would prefer to spend his life in conversation. For Curt, besides the production of efficient and aesthetic objects, civilization meant idleness or leisure, time to think, converse, reflect and pursue intellectual and sensual objectives. He admired hard work and human intelligence, but he admired human intelligence applied to technological innovation to save labour more than anything else. During the times of the hippie uprisings, Curt was unique: instead of denouncing and abhorring technological change and technology itself, he embraced it as a mode of achieving vast social change and human freedom. I have always remembered his comment about the ephemeral and poetic beauty of the operation of the automobile engine as a representation of the power of human consciousness and creativity.

It was Curt's self-appointed and self-chosen role to be at odds with everything. He was a rebel not only against the established order, but also against the modes of opposition that were taken as rebellion in those days. When others were turning to psychedelic drugs, Curt remained loyal to alcohol as a means of achieving if not mental liberation, at least a different state of mind, and argued persistently and consistently against the use of drugs by his friends, scoffing at the idea that drugs could bring enlightenment or even open minds. It might easily be understood that Curt was at odds not only with the individuals and institutions of the establishment, but also with the disestablishmentarians of the time. People of the anti-institutional artistic underground were both intrigued by him and exasperated by him from time to time, but his opinions and views could never be easily ignored, because they were always intelligently worked out, eloquently and creatively expressed, and more often than not, much less shallow than the prevailing views sponsored in the media and other official circles.

Curt was not in the foreground of artistic production, publicity or what not. But he wasn't ever invisible either. He and his group were influential both directly and indirectly because they were active in the arts. Some of them are now well known as underground artists of that period and some of them are even now emerging into a kind of aboveground respectability. John Newlove, a Governor General's award winning poet was part of Curt's circle, as was Roy Kiyooka, who has posthumously assumed a place as one of Vancouver's premier artists of the 1960s as well. Al Neil, known then as a be-bop pianist, later reincarnated as a writer and performance artist, and still later as a collagist and visual artist, was also part of the group. The unsung Fred Douglas, who may yet be more widely recognized on the basis of his emerging work, was part of that group too. As I said, their presence was consistently characterized by their unrelentingly critical stance, and this had a profound influence throughout the social life of the germinal art movement of Vancouver in the 1960s. Curt's views had significant influence within this group, and the group's views had a definite osmotic influence in the artistic and the broader cultural community at large around it. And because their stance was the most developed critical attitude of their time, their influence on the cultural development of Vancouver was probably the most decisive of the period.

Published in *West Coast Line* 47 – Vol. 39 No.2. 2005 ISSN-4271.
Co-published with Presentation House Gallery ISBN 0-920293-67-0

RED LANE

Red Lane Awake

In the back room of the apartment, whose walls were literally made of cardboard painted black, my clothes were scattered helter-skelter on the floor. For a time, there was no bed back there, and I slept in a nest of my discarded clothing, while Red slept in the living room. More often than not, I rose earlier than he did. I suspected that he stayed up later after I had gone to bed, worrying over secret projects of his own, preparing and plotting his numerous surprises, a late night alchemist and trickster.

Beyond the morning gloom of the hallway outside my room, the living room was resplendent with a nimbus of blinding dawn light, made more rich and subtle by the dust that floated in glowing fragments in the air.

Within the kitchen, there were sounds. Barefoot, quietly, I approached the door. Red was standing over the stove with acute attention, preparing eggs in a frying pan. I waited by the door to see if he would notice me, but his eyes remained resolutely fixed on his task. Grasping the handle of the frying pan with his left hand, he half-turned his back and face, working deliberately and patiently with a kitchen knife held in his right hand, neatening the edges of the eggs. For once, I thought, I might prepare a surprise for him, catch him unawares. Yet there was something too deliberate about his movements, the way his eyes turned everywhere except toward the doorway where I stood — a kind of tension in his posture, as though he knew he was being observed.

I sneaked down the hallway to the living room and peered again into the kitchen from its other door. Carefully, Red worked his eggs, now separating their edges from the pan with his knife. In the Air Force, he had been a cook, and George Bowering had told me how he had been able to hold two eggs in each hand, cracking them briskly, first one hand, and then the other, before easing them precisely and neatly into position on the grill where a dozen or more of them were frying all together in the fat, then one by one in neat and patterned gestures, slipping them onto plates along with bacon and potatoes and passing them through the window of the galley to feed the newly-wakened airmen.

The neatness and perfection with which he performed even the smallest tasks was a source of pride to him. Even small failures—a darkened, ragged edge, a broken yoke, would disappoint him, evoking grimaces of exaggerated comic disgust. He liked to be watched at these tasks, like a stage magician— in his bearing a calculated insouciance, a devil-may-care indifference, the ironic self-confidence of the clown-juggler—the possibility of utter failure and astonishing success balanced with precarious precision.

I watched him from the doorway, waiting for his pose to break. He turned slightly in one direction, and then again in the other direction, slightly. There was a conscious deliberation in every move he made, teasing me, perhaps, keeping me always in doubt as to whether he was aware of my presence or not. Then suddenly there was no longer any doubt. He stopped in mid-activity, leaned forward, stood still as a statue for the fraction of a second, staring through the other door I had abandoned. Then, as though agitated by a crazy impulse, began a mad little dance to the music of the radio, pumping arms and elbows, knees and neck, pivoting his bent body in awkward, yet perfect, right angles back and forth on the floor, whistling through his teeth, in a trick that only he knew how to perform. As soon as the dance began, it ended. He went back to neatening his eggs, not once looking in my direction. Abject, admiring, I went and sat down in the living room and waited.

Moments later, he emerged with his eggs on a plate. "Good morning, Mr. Reid," he said, and sitting down on his bed of cushions, salted and peppered his eggs, and enjoyed his breakfast without another word.

Looking out the window to the sunny morning, I saw the weeds in the backyard, the dandelions winking up at me.

Red Lane Asleep

It occurred to me that Red Lane asleep is different from Red Lane awake. All the loose, angular energy of his muscles and his bones is missing, the subtle electricity of his pale, freckled skin, his unique quick invulnerability. He sleeps on his back in the living room on three sofa cushions for which there is no sofa. His head is crooked backward over the end of a cushion, mouth opened wide, knees incongruously bent. He looks as though he might be snoring, but he isn't. He is silent, unmoving. No hint of breathing disturbs his inert presence.

He sleeps in the bright soft sunlight of the early morning. A man who when awake is so aware, is now so distant, so unseeing. There is the sudden strange suspicion that he isn't really sleeping, he's only feigning sleep. In the flash of a moment, that sprung collection of bones and flesh will drag itself together, leap to its feet and look around, and then begin some crazy, gimcrack monologue to launch the morning. But he only goes on sleeping. And now at last I see his breathing, a slow ticking through his nose and mouth, a tiny rise in the sunken fish-white abdomen, a slight rise and tilt at the bottom of his rib cage. He is alive.

His nakedness is too extreme. The scrap of underwear he's wearing, old and grey, is hanging loosely from the bottom of his belly and his thighs. The flesh of his body is hanging loose around his bones; the bottom of his rib cage thrusts upward against that sagging, downward-drawn flesh. The outline of his ribs is too visible, beneath the ribs the hint of quiescent organs, the liver, the heart, the pink lungs. The brain, so active when awake, now seems empty, even of the hint of a dream. His veins show purple on his skin, an entirely different hue from when he is awake. The quick alabaster of his skin is gone — there is a grey translucence to it. He reminds me of the featherless small birds in the nests of robins, blind infant mice, things on the verge, on the edge of life and death, things newly dead or newly born.

When other people sleep, their cares drift off their faces. They appear as they appeared when they were children, smooth-faced, uninjured. On the sleeping face and body of Red Lane is printed the trauma of being newly-born, or the weight of heavy, painful years, the touching sadness of the aged. You want to cover that nakedness, to warm it, to bring it colour, and yet to let it sleep, as though the sleep is necessary because the sadness that is in him while he is awake is now no longer hidden, no longer driven under, but is allowed its place. If sleep, as the poets have said, is the simulacrum of death, then Red's death is seeping out of him while he lies asleep, so that when he wakens, he can be alive and steadfast again, so that he can carry the day.

"Red Lane Asleep" was originally published in *I, Another, The Space Between*, Talonbooks Ltd. 2004.

RED AND SAM

At first we used to sleep in late. Stay up until the wee hours drinking and talking and then wake up leaden and sodden at noon the next day. We would only be taking our first cups of instant coffee when Sam Perry would burst into the apartment fresh from his morning adventure, preening with enthusiasm, shouting, laughing, slicing up oranges with a knife and preparing a late morning feast for us, describing his adventure on his little motorbike, the flow of light on the buildings as he rode through the city with no one else on the streets, down to the beaches, into the park, the flow of wind and light in the trees. "Get up early, boys, that's the way to do it. You can write, you can photograph, you can look at things, and by noon time, you've already done a whole bunch of stuff, and the afternoon is still there for some more. There's too much life around to spend it sleeping."

At first we used to mutter and complain, but soon enough we envied him and then admired him and finally imitated him and began to rise early, too. We became a household of early risers. No matter how late we stayed up the night before, we tried to rise by eight o'clock and begin the day. We found that Sam was not the hero we thought he was when we began to wake up along with him. He was on his feet, all right, but he wasn't with us. He was like a zombie, staring dumbly into space, chewing the cud of his morosity like an old man.

The coffee would be ready, and the oranges, but when we would ask him if he wanted any, he would only stare stupidly away, ignoring us and saying nothing. We got used to his early morning funk just as we got used to his bursts of enthusiasm later in the day. It usually took him about an hour to really come to life, and as soon as he was ready, he would burst away out the door without having exchanged as much as ten words with us. Often, he stayed the night away and didn't return until noon. He was madly in love with the woman he would soon marry, but she was unsure of his bohemian ways, his boyish refractory willfulness, and the more she expressed her doubts about him and turned away from him, the more madly and inventively he pursued her, bringing her flowers late at night, showing up at parties with other women, and then dragging her away with him, professing his mad love.

Finally, in a last desperate effort to escape him, she signed up to go to northern India on a rescue project for Tibetan refugees. When he begged her tearfully and lyrically to let him go along, she finally relented, because even if, in her mind, he was crazy, he was infinitely more interesting and full of life than any thousand other men she might have married. Propriety demanded that if they were to travel as a couple, they had to be legally married, and so they were, all in the space of two weeks, and then they were gone to northern India, where they later had an audience with his Holiness, the Dalai Lama.

Their later relationship turned out to be one of the most mournful in the history of the Vancouver poets and writers of those days, but that is another story. The story of Red Lane and Sam Perry are linked because their living energy exerted a huge influence on the other writers around them, because both died tragically early, and because each of their deaths, in its own way, sent terrible shock waves through the ranks of our tenuous community.

th pome wuz a storee nd is th storee: th erlee daze uv blewointment

In a way, it has always been pointless to talk about bill bissett's past. His work in poetry, painting and performance art has always pointed toward the living present and toward the future, never toward the dead past. While others change and adapt, compromise and take on new public personae, bill bissett seems only to emerge as more and more of what he was before, as though perfecting and protecting an original image of himself. His program has never changed: from the beginning, his work in every genre has aimed to mobilize the crudest, simplest, oldest and most primitive pictorial and verbal techniques to invoke a state of mind and being that he calls "ecstatic yunyun," the linking of the phenomenal and the transcendental world, the vulgar and the celestial, the earthly and the heavenly. This semi-mystical pursuit has been expressed in one of his constantly recurring graphic images: two faces, one male, the other female, turn toward each other in the impending moment of an ecstatic kiss, hot and sexual on one hand and full of aching spirituality on the other. In this sense, he is the inheritor of the romantic tradition of Hollywood as much as that of William Blake.

The wild bohemian bill bissett was before the Beatles and Bob Dylan, a beatnik, a real one, and really here in Vancouver. In those days of the early 1960s, he seemed strange, almost otherworldly, a kind of alien. Now he seems the most familiar of them all. hard 2 beeleev.

Not nostalgia, nor even objective memory, can ever unearth or replay the terror and dismay we all felt during those times of the late 1950s and early 1960s when the threat of nuclear annihilation was always concretely present to our bodies and our minds. We lived every day and dreamed every night in fear that the city might actually be incinerated, the entire earth of people wasted and destroyed. These nightmares are played and replayed in bill's poetry of the time, and in the work of all the rest of us, too. Easy now to forget that Hiroshima was right close by in time and history and there were plenty of current reminders that it could happen again: the Cuban missile crisis of 1962, the assassination of President Kennedy in 1963, and later the new holocaust of Vietnam, the burnings in Watts and Detroit. They didn't happen here in Vancouver, Canada, but they made us sit up and take notice, added a chemistry of desperation to our young lives—a sense of mission, because we felt we had to act to save the future, but also a sense of recklessness, because there might not be a future despite all our utopian efforts.

Of all the people who came forward to make art their life in those days, bill and some of his friends were the farthest out, the strangest, the ones whose rebellion and rejection of established order was most complete. The first time I actually spoke to bill bissett was in 1959, when I was still in high-school, finishing grade thirteen at King Edward, now burned out of existence. Through *Time* magazine and my mother's literary curiosity, I had already encountered the work of Jack Kerouac and Allen Ginsberg, spent weekend evenings at the little beatnik clubs that began to spring up in Vancouver in imitation of the real thing in New York and San Francisco: the Black Spot, the Cellar, the Inquisition, the Flat Five, The Den, Goof's Pad—the names say it all.

bill was seen in all of them, a highly visible and distinctive presence. I knew who he was before I really met him. I wanted to know him better, because he seemed the embodiment of the truly hip, a real Ginsberg, a real Kerouac, right here in Vancouver. In those very early days, he was a strange, shy, fey, gaunt youth, with the haunted look of a recent runaway or escapee, somehow loose and nervous at the same time. His expression then, as now, slipped between a sleepy, cat-like sensuality and a kind of surprised bemusement, eyebrows up, lips slightly parted. He sometimes wore a charcoal suit with stove-pipe pants, and looked to me for all the world like the poet in the drawing on the cover of a popular paperback anthology of modern French verse, sensitive, starved, ragged.

Because he was so different from everyone else in those days, he was the subject of quite a lot of gossip and comment. Rumour said he came from Halifax, that he was from what was reverentially called "a good family," that he was openly bi-sexual, at a time when the life of open homosexuality was not only forbidden, but truly dangerous. There were scary but also intriguing rumors: bill mainlined heroin, I heard, and believed it when it was also said he had even mainlained novocaine. I couldn't imagine the effect it might have had, apart from total body numbness. With his ambiguous sexual orientation, his purported drug use, and his politics, which, if not outrightly communist, were in any case very far to the left, bill bissett managed to embody within his own single person, everything officially stigmatised as dangerous and radical. And yet, to my officially-trained right-out-of-high-school eye, bill bissett radiated an attractive angelic insouciance, a palpable aura of sweet charisma.

In my imagination, bill was the product of the original Vancouver Bohemia, the one that was rooted in downtown Robson Street, the real early Bohemia, not the American-media-created Bohemia, the so-called "counter-culture" of Fourth Avenue that emerged after the middle 1960s, though bill was raging at the centre of that later movement, too. Robson Street in the late 1950s and early 1960s was definitely not the realm of bright, upscale boutiques and cosmopolitanism it has now become. Instead, it was the old existentialist pre- and post-war Europe, a grey and dingy, somehow exotic and exciting collection of decaying shops and restaurants, owned and run by German and East European immigrants—"DPs" as they were labeled then. These "displaced persons" had experienced directly the reality of world wars, seen both communism and fascism first hand, understood politics and its horrors in ways we never could. The people who lived on the street seemed to me dark, cranky, world-weary, or alternatively strange, shy, and frightened. They seemed to live with the realization that their condition and presence was precarious and fraught with hidden danger. bill seemed able to find acceptance within their circles easily—a kind of wraith, neither of their world nor of mine. He knew people whose names were Ivan, Valdemar, Gudrun, Birgit, and seemed naturally in his element among them.

bill bissett was always associated in my mind with a wistfully melancholy little man who ran a tiny egg store on Robson Street. With his sad and knowing gaze, the little man looked unnervingly like Peter Lorre. Day after day, he sat gazing out onto the street, waiting for customers, I supposed, though I never saw anybody in the store besides the man himself. A single small sign in the window, which displayed no visible goods for sale, read "Cracks: 39¢ doz." Who would buy cracks, I wondered, and what were they anyway?

Milton Acorn once shyly intimated to me his weird conviction that some of the shops along Robson Street seemed to appear and disappear mysteriously, unaccountably changing places in the street from day to day and overnight. I knew exactly what he meant: I had often felt similar crazy intimations. Now the whole of the old Robson Street has disappeared, but behind the new facades, the erased faces of the old shops keep peering out, like the multitudinous human and animal faces hidden in a bill bissett landscape.

And so it was too with the little shop and the sad little Peter Lorre in its window. The egg man's character, when I finally met him, was like one side of bill bissett's—mild, sweet, kindly, almost saintly in an old world way. bill was like him in other ways, too. He seemed to unaccountably appear and disappear. Where you might expect to find him, he wouldn't be. Then suddenly and unexpectedly, he would be there, in a completely unexpected place, crammed into a corner at a party, or waiting outside a laundromat for his clothes to finish drying. In those days, you couldn't imagine he would ever actually carry out any merely practical thing like that. Beatniks lived in the spirit world and never did their laundry. They simply wore the same clothes always until they fell off their bodies, I supposed, and then found new ones. But there he would be, nonetheless, outside the laundromat, waiting for his clothes to dry. Once I told him I had to look for a job. "Oh, that's too bad," he said, deep sympathy vibrating in his voice. Another time, imbued with the notion popular among Canadian intellectuals at the time that American movies were an inferior, even a destructive, form of culture, I asked him how he could stand to watch so many movies. He told me he sometimes viewed as many as three movies a day, sometimes three times a week, and made no distinction between American commercial movies and European "art" movies. "Oh, it's cool, you know," he explained, "Everything becomes, like, the same after a while." And that made a kind of sense to me.

It's hard to remember the depth of the cultural wasteland in Vancouver of those days. There was the Vancouver Public Library, UBC, the Art School and the Art Gallery. Our only contact with European culture was through the Cinema 16 program at the University, and free lunch-time concerts of the full cycle of Beethoven Quartets, which were attended on at least one occasion by a delegation of bearded beatniks from the Art School headed by Roy Kiyooka, and with him Curt Lang, Fred Douglas, Judy Copithorne—the "downtown" poets—all wearing youthful looks of world-weariness and scorn for us university intellectuals. The Art Gallery's most important room in those days was the permanent Emily Carr collection, which seemed to have been put together by someone who construed Emily as a kind of frontier Van Gogh, all schizophrenic swirls and spirals, quite dizzying in fact. To enter the room was to be thrown into a kind of vertigo, which would remain even after you had escaped into the street. The rest of culture was taken up by Izzy's, The Cave, The Penthouse, a distant night-club sophistication and phoniness, which we, in our customary indigence, could never afford. There was one (one!) commercial art gallery dedicated to contemporary (or at least, modernist) painting. Friday evenings we went there to view the latest opening: Roy Kiyooka, Claude Breeze, Jack Shadbolt, B.C. Binning, Gordon Smith, Takao Tanabe, Audrey Capel Doray,

Peter Aspell. We went there to meet each other and to suck up the cheap free wine and food, later in the evening adjourning to the Georgia and the Cecil, staying until closing time, then buying cases of beer and driving to all-night parties in private houses, returning home with the first appearance of dawn in the sky.

Once, before I knew him very well, I witnessed bill in the midst of a poetry reading at the Cellar, a legendary jazz club in the dim alley behind Doug Hepburn's gym at Broadway and Main. Poetry and jazz together was big those days. Jack Kerouac himself had appeared on television accompanied by Steve Allen's piano. Local genius and bebop pianist Al Neil accompanied Kenneth Patchen in a pioneer example of the genre recorded at the Cellar, still one of the best around, both for its music and its poetry. The Cellar really was a cellar — a cold concrete floor, low ceilings, a permanent dusty darkness inside. Men went there after the bars had closed, carrying brown bags filled with whiskey bottles. There, they bought ice and ginger-ale at inflated prices, and talked drunkenly over the sounds of local and visiting jazz artists, drinking until 2 am in exciting semi-legality.

bill that night was perched unsteadily on a narrow, wobbling formica table, looking ragged and vulnerable, reading his poems in a breathless, high, feminine voice. The place was filled with drunk and hateful males, men in their thirties and forties, who began yelling the worst insults they knew, inspired by their deepest homophobic fears: "Fruit!" "Queer!" "Fairy!" Then they began throwing things. A piece of hurled crockery struck bill's cheekbone, drawing a drop of blood. By a kind of fatal synchronicity, the next line of bill's poem was "I want to kill you!" bill read the line with full venomous volume, drawing hoots of ugly laughter. I was surprised and impressed with the sudden venom and rage in bill's response. I had always thought he was a gentle and completely retiring soul, but had not reckoned with the Scorpio side of his birth sign, on the cusp of Sagittarius, and that combined with the doubleness of Gemini rising. I admired bill that night even while despising my own cowardice for regarding his hot courage as merely foolhardy. From that moment, I understood that underneath the soft and pacifist exterior that bill bissett shows to the world, there lies a core of hard steel, an unbelievable stubbornness and brave anger. Without that core of stubbornness, it would have been impossible for bill to have lived the kind of life he has sustained, now going on for well over fifty years.

First he lived in the West End—the old West End of huge old decaying blue houses, dark rented rooms surrounded by the seashore on all sides. The first time I remember visiting him was one of those ominous dark and gusty February Vancouver days, full of rain and penetrating damp. I went to view his manuscripts with the aim of selecting some poems for TISH, in which I was a contributing editor. bill was there with Judy Copithorne, and someone else, my memory fails me, probably Martina Clinton, bill's partner of those days. Martina was a dark, seemingly sullen and mysterious presence, often silent, who sometimes broke out in excited utterances of startling eloquence and insight. bill placed a ragged pile of manuscripts two feet high on the floor in front of me.

"Can't you choose some poems for me?" I asked, at a loss. He reached into the pile completely at random and pulled out two or three poems. "How about these ones?" He hadn't even looked at them, and after I read them, I was unable to find anything to distinguish them from any of the other poems in the pile. bill asked me what I thought I might be looking for. I said I simply wanted some of the poems bill himself might regard as his best, or at least "good" poems. "But how will I know?" he asked, with what seemed to me a maddening mixture of ingenuousness and cunning.

Years of later experience have taught me that bill really does not make distinctions between the "good" or the less good in art or in life. It is all only experience to him, his constant effort being always to make two different worlds cohere: the world of ordinary daily grime and ugliness, of "real life" and hardship on one hand and the inner, celestial, spiritual world of sunshine, stars and flowers on the other hand, to effect a Blake-like ecstatic "yunyun." His publication *blewointment*, like his iconic paintings and his poetry, was simply one more material instrument for creating that human connection—ragged, improvised, ink-smeared. At first sight bafflingly various, the succeeding issues of *blewointment* gradually brought the magazine into focus as the product of bill bissett's vision and engagement with his own social world, his effort to sponsor creative efforts of all kinds within the living context of the city and its artistic community. He carried copies with him everywhere, constantly exercising his patient skills as a salesman, explaining to anyone and everyone the importance of making financial contributions necessary to the survival of *blewointment*, and consequently to the very survival of the Vancouver arts community.

bpNichol once wrote that *blewointment* was "...more interested in the news than in preserving great literature." This is as true as anything ever said about bill bissett and his work. His poems, paintings, chants, prayers and performances, like his daily acts, appear only as individual events in an on-going life process and its work. Ideas of "good, better, best," simply don't apply. This is one of the reasons why there is little use in talking about "influence" in bissett' work. He has been "influenced" and affected by everything valuable in modern art and literature: Picasso, Joyce, Stein, Whitman and Blake, Emily Carr, the movies, and literally all of his artistic contemporaries—the works and deeds of his entire vast circle of friends and well-wishers. And his enemies and persecutors, too—the police, the judges, the prosecutors, the politicians, and the bankers and businessmen they protect, as well as the literary establishment, frosty professorial poets, fat-cat poets and impresarios who labelled his anti-establishment politics as "mere paranoia."

bill and his friends seemed to move around the city like birds, finding first one nest and then another. It seems to me today strangely appropriate that hardly any of the houses in which bill bissett ever lived still exist on earth. Most of these ramshackle structures have all disappeared in the new Vancouver, like most of the ephemeral copies of the original *blewointment*. It wasn't difficult in those days for any of us to move around: none of us possessed enough worldly goods to make moving house a very heavy chore.

The next time I remember visiting bill, he was living on the east side of Burrard Street, the southern foot of Hornby Street, when it was still a residential area. I remember only a vast space on the bottom floor. Its walls and ceiling were painted extravagantly in shiny enamel black. There was no floor, only damp, bare musty-smelling earth. The place seemed to me like an anthracite cave. I feared that bill and his friends who lived there would succumb to tuberculosis or pneumonia, like Nova Scotia miners, or natives in the North. bill was already afflicted with a deep bronchial cough. Typically, though, he was ecstatically enthusiastic about these new lodgings, exclaiming raptly about the beauty of the shaft of sunlight entering the gloom from the door opening onto the field of weeds outside.

Later, he lived with his partner, Martina Clinton, in various places around Fourth Avenue, but especially, the huge warehouse studio space on the bottom floor of the building on the corner of Yew and York in Kitsalano, later occupied by the artist, Gordon Payne. Upstairs at various times lived Gerry Geisler and his wife, John and Susan Newlove, and, in the other apartment in the same building, Gladys Hindmarch. Within a block or two and at various times, the apartments and suites were occupied by George and Angela Bowering, Gary Lee Nova, David Shiletto, Rick Kataieff and his wife Anne, Marcia Stone. Roy Kiyooka, Jack Wise, David Mayrs and dozens of others lived within walking distance. It was common in those days for people simply to wander through the neighbourhood, visiting their friends, looking at new poems, new paintings, collages—whatever was being produced. bill's huge and draughty downstairs warehouse studio with its heaving floors, was the site of many loud ecstatic parties. I cannot begin to name all the people who came there, but I do remember one night responding to a knock on the door to encounter the smiling and quite radiant presence of Margaret Atwood.

It's astonishing now to look back over the issues of *blewointment*, read the tables of contents and see the names of so many now well-known, even outrageously famous Canadian writers and poets in its pages: Al Purdy, Earle Birney, Margaret Avison, Milton Acorn, Dorothy Livesay, Pat Lowther, Margaret Atwood, Michael Ondaatje, George Bowering, Eli Mandel, Colleen Thibaudeau, Red Lane, Pat Lane, John Newlove, Gerry Gilbert, Robert Hogg, Roy Kiyooka, Carole Fisher, Brian Fisher, Al Neil, Seymour Mayne, C.H. Gervais, Barry McKinnon, Mina Forsyth, Gladys Hindmarch, Judy Copithorne, Maxine Gadd, Susan Musgrave, Gwen Hauser, Steve McCaffery, bpNichol, Nelson Ball, David UU, Colin Browne, Andrew Suknaski, Scott Watson, Robert Zend, Carolyn Zonailo: all names which have continued to appear with new poems in current literary journals throughout the continent, and have made unique contributions to the cultural life of the country. There are, besides, the names of many lesser-known, but still well-remembered Vancouver personalities and their valuable poems: Lanny Beckman, p.x. belinsky, Charles Boylan, John Burton, David Cull, Lance Farrell, Jock Hearn, Peter Hlookoff, Neap Hoover, Martin Jensen, Curt Lang, Scott Lawrence, Joy Long, Rosemary Hollingshead, Shirl Jackson, Dennis Jackson, Beth Jancola, Doug Mawhinney, Jack Mawhinney, Jerry Matsubishi, Beth Perry, David Phillips, Dallas Selman, Beverley Simons, Colin Stuart, Robby Sutherland, Roger Tentrey, George Vagenas. These names may have disappeared from the public eye, but the poems and stories that bill published over their names still resonate and still speak and call to mind the excitement, energy and joyful camaraderie of those days, when we all still believed that the world could really be changed, and that our own activity was relevant to the future. I want to name them all, because they all had a part in making the city what it was then, and in an underground way, what it remains today.

In those days, the later-to-be-famous-and-successful were still the not-yet-successful and the little-known. It was generally recognized, of course, that Al Purdy and Milton Acorn were great Canadian poets, and that John Newlove and Margaret Atwood were rising stars. But we all met with each other on the streets and houses of the city as equals—person to person, without the protocol and distance that was bound to come later. Artists who become famous as Margaret Atwood has, are quite properly compelled to take on public personae and habits that protect them and their creative lives from the demands of a voracious celebrity-hungry public. But in those days, they were simply Peggy, Al, John and bill, fellow residents of the neighbourhood or the city, literary and artistic fellow-travellers. bill has steadily maintained the same public persona, and has developed a repertoire of deliberate devices to smooth situations and to create a visible aura which allows for both opening to exchanges of intimacy and the protection of his own personal security and privacy. His typical greeting: "Lightning and magic rainbows. Are you raging?" is one of these devices, a way of achieving a stability of personality, remaining recognizable, but recognizably different, through time and space. He is, all the same, probably the least private of any public or semi-public figure—now as then, he is available to anyone at all, in his poems as in his life. He is always ready to speak without reserve to practically any unthreatening stranger he encounters on the street, from the most opulent to the most abject.

Like that other famous dadaist Kurt Schwitters, people at first find bill strange, but soon become conscious of his harmlessness and his good will, easily become accustomed to him, fall into conversation, exchanging observations, easy intimacies and confidences just as if they had been friends for ages, or as if they had discovered a new friend who for once allows them to speak freely and without reserve. His gift for momentarily liberating the inner lives of strangers seems to work on almost everybody.

bill is a complete democrat in his social habits, makes no prejudiced assumptions about any human being in advance. His meeting with the Queen is a hilarious example: Susan Musgrave reports that bill, dressed in pale purple tuxedo and a purple ruffled shirt, told the Queen she was much prettier in person than her pictures on the dollar bill, and later complimented her, "You look smashing in yellow, Your Majesty." The mental image of the two of them together, tête-à-tête, Elizabeth the Queen in her yellow frock and bill the gentle fool in his violet tuxedo, is a ravishing one. I hope there is a photograph somewhere, or better, even a film of this ineffable moment. Carol Bolt tells the story of slipping out to have a pee while waiting impatiently for the Queen's arrival, returning moments later only to view the Queen and her retinue rushing away from her out of the hall. Spying Carol's crushed disappointment, gallant bill in his purple tuxedo immediately sped down the hallway to catch Her Majesty up. Oblivious to every protocol which forbids mere subjects from daring to touch the sacred body of the monarch, bill caught the Queen from behind by her shoulder, breathlessly exclaiming, "Your Majesty, Your Majesty, Carol wanted to meet you!" Carol said the entire security corps went stiff as statues, ready to seize poor bill and tear him to pieces. Unfazed, the Queen graciously halted the procession long enough to shake Carol's hand—surely sweat-moistened by now, and only said to Carol, "Oh, yes, I did so want to meet you," and then regally passed on.

To my mind, this moment typifies the poetic persona of bill bissett: he is the perfect image of "The Fool" of the Tarot, the young man who steps smiling into the abyss of the unknown, the purest kind of poet and individual bill bissett was and remains. bissett's childlikeness is the result of a decision taken as an adult, a role which he strives to grow out of or back to or through to.

> *"We listened to Ornette Coleman a lot, Mingus,*
> *Al Neil—and got into a lot of trouble, hard times."*

Not all was joyousness and light and foolery in those days, or even during, the years of hippie "peace and love." There was plenty of tragedy and darkness, too. Michael Coutts, a talented and disturbed young poet and bill's close friend, died of a heroin overdose at the age of 21. Red Lane, Pat Lane's older brother and a major influence on Pat's life and poetry, died suddenly of a brain aneurysm in 1964. Sam Perry, a young man of huge energies and intelligence, a scientist, an athlete, a highly creative film-maker and writer, the organizer of the original Vancouver Trips Festival, shot himself in his studio in 1966 and sent the entire community into shock and crisis. Neri, Maxine Gadd's younger brother, jumped off the Burrard Bridge. bill knew all of these people personally, and was extremely close to Red and Sam and Michael. These tragic local events blended with the apocalyptical confusion of the times, so those days were lived with a sense of loss and darkness that would not go away. We argued and talked incessantly amongst each other, about what was hip and what was not hip, what was Zen and unZen, about violent versus non-violent resistance in politics, the limits of the sexual revolution, drugs, friendship, money, the importance or non-importance of this or that artist, this or that school of poetry, art or music, the relationship of politics to art, anarchy vs. structure, form vs. content, the necessity for crafted form versus unrestrained spontaneity, etc., etc.

Our utopian hopes were finally crushed by the activities of the local authorities, who were unrelenting those days in their harassment and intimidation of key members of the rebellious community of youth. bill bissett was one of its leaders, and therefore the target of a long campaign of surveil-lance, harassment, beatings and intimidation. bill's home was invaded many times by the violent representatives of the law, who finally succeeded in arresting him and sending him to prison in 1968 for marijuana possession. Among the many poems that document and comment upon these events is one written while bill was in the Oakalla Prison Farm in January, 1969:

either way, as if what yu decide
to feel determines th turns
taken of such blinding flow

who dusint lie as especially
(liberal) indignation becums

an impossibility, when
as life/death is also absurdity,
yu sit behind bars, turning to
endless vapors, huh

heres that crook again back
home, just wait'l i get to
scoop him twice

it's all one school, and if (learn, nut)
yu are aggressive so are the screws
so, cool it, we're all part of this

historical mistake, even love
may now be possible, tho, don't
hold yr breath, be seein' ya,

mother earth

both th prosecutor at th last sentencing nd
Louis Dudek at th Poets Conference in T.O.
sd if he's any good as a poet he'l write just

as well inside jail as on th street:
i think this is a lousy pome,
what do yu think, shit-head reader.

where do you think yu are, heaven (already)

These events, to my mind, closed a chapter in the history of resistance by the Vancouver artistic community to the power of established authority. We became aware that something more than utopian idealism would be required to break that power. bill's later struggle with the philistines of the House of Commons, who attacked his work as part of an all-round attack on government funding for the arts, belongs to a separate chapter, and is another story and another poem. That later attack was in fact the most signal honour of bill bissett's career, and deserves a special treatment.

NOTES: Part of the title, and some of the subtitles and quotes in this article have been taken from an interview with bill bissett by Barry McKinnon entitled *blewointment*, (*Open Letter*, Seventh Series, Nos. 2-3: Summer-Fall 1988). Grateful thanks to Gene Bridwell and Charles Watts of the Special Collections Library at Simon Fraser University, the current site of the most complete collection of the publications of blewointment. I would also like to acknowledge the contribution of Karl Jirgens' very thoroughgoing article called "bill bissett" which appears in *Canadian Writers and Their Works: Poetry Series*, Volume 8 (ECW Press, Toronto, 1992), and especially for his treatment of bill's concept of "ecstatic yunyun."

---

th pome wuz a storee nd is th storee: th erlee daze uv blewointment was originally published in *The Capilano Review* issue 2.23, Fall 1997.

BOB DYLAN

On March 26, 1966, Bob Dylan led his band into our west coast Canadian city of Vancouver for a concert in front of a full house of 5,000 fans at the Agrodome, the city's largest public venue at the time. It was to be the last concert he would perform in North America for eight long years. Dylan had already been canonized by the media for a new generation of youthful believers as a singing troubadour of their rebellious aspirations to an all-encompassing social revolution. Young adults and teenagers throughout the world were listening to his recordings raptly, as if they were the holy writ of their own social and political awakening, conducting exercises in exegesis to decipher the esoteric code of their new religion's ethos.

The new youthful rebellion found its expression in a creative explosion within American pop music, first and most notably through Bob Dylan who had been attracted to New York's Greenwich Village Beat scene in 1960. Having just moved to the vanguard of the acoustic folk music revival of the labour and civil rights movements with his anthem "The Times They Are A Changin'" in 1963, to the consternation of his fans he had gone electric when the British Invasion landed on the beachhead of the *Ed Sullivan Show* that same year. From there, the Beatles' and the Rolling Stones' cynical notes of social criticism had begun to sweep the formerly bland pap of American commercial pop music to the sidelines of cool.

Unknown to his explosively widening audience at the time, Dylan himself was in the midst of a profound personal crisis invoked by his reaction to his own sudden celebrity, ironically engineered and manufactured by those who were closest to him: his managers and nearest business associates.

On that grey and drizzling March evening, five of us—self-styled poets and artists all—were driving east along Vancouver's Hastings Street in Peter Auxier's beaten up dark blue Chevy. The goal of our pilgrimage was Bob Dylan's Vancouver concert later that night. Fervent anticipation beat in our hearts. Like thousands of other teenagers and young adults, we looked to Dylan as our exalted comrade, a poet-herald of the future in the cultural war we all believed in, and dreamed we were waging together with the rest of our generation against the dark, conformist past that even president Eisenhower had warned against as he stepped down from the American presidency: the military industrial complex—colloquially known as The Man. A significant portion of our generation was steaming up to full rebellion against the established public order that surrounded us, an order that in our eyes threatened the future of the entire planet with atomic wars to perpetuate its world of permanent social and racial inequality.

The five of us in the car regarded ourselves as precocious veteran cognoscenti of the counter-cultural revolution which had first sprung into existence in the late 1950s, nourished on the example of American cultural phenomena, including modern jazz and the literary florescence of the Beat generation. Most of us would be present to see and hear Charles Olson at the 1963 Vancouver poetry conference expounding on his magic mushroom experience with the not quite yet world famous psychedelic guru Timothy Leary at Harvard. From the mouths of Olson, Allen Ginsberg, Robert Creeley, Margaret Avison and other poets at that conference, we heard the prophesy of the impending seismic shift in North American consciousness emerging from the increasingly electrifying movements within the American society and body politic.

It's no exaggeration to say that we all saw ourselves as situated close to the very centre—perhaps even on the vanguard—of that world-wide counter-cultural movement in our own city, and had done so even before the earliest days of Dylan's growing celebrity.

In our own minds, we were already part of the cultural awakening of which our comrade, our companion, our brother in arms Bob Dylan was emerging in the media as our spokesman. Despite the mental confusion, contradiction and uncertainty inevitably engendered by the arrival of any new consciousness, we believed ourselves sublimely hip, wise and knowledgeable about all that was going on in the world, including what was going on with our recently anointed populist hero. We admired Dylan as a poet and an avatar of a new world being born out of the collective mouths and activities of our generation—as one of us.

Perhaps most important of all, we saw our own cultural and intellectual roots in what had been popularly known in the 1950s as the Beat Generation era, which we regarded as intellectually deeper than the new, counter-culture movement of the post-war baby boom generation. We saw the so-called hippie movement among our slightly younger peers as a new wave of what our own generation, born just before or during the Second World War, had inaugurated—as a popular movement less deeply intellectual than that of our earlier initiatives. Dylan, born in 1941, seemed to us a worthy and above all legitimate follower of the poet Allen Ginsberg, and activist folk singers Woody Guthrie and Pete Seeger. And for a while, it's true, even we were enthralled by the hypnotic jingles of the Beatles, who had managed to divert our attention briefly from the complexities and subtleties of the jazz which had been the greatest formative influence on our emotional lives.

Carol and my companions on that day were all people who had been part of the Vancouver counter-culture movement from the very beginning of the sixties. It was a phenomenon still little known to the wider public, yet increasingly popular at the time to the minority communities advocating public cultural action in the city, and particularly among the youth of the city. Peter Auxier, then a poet, was driving the car. He was later to become one of the forgotten founders of *The Georgia Straight*, the main media organ of the Vancouver underground when it was founded a year later. Mitzi Gibbs, a wise and sparkling personality, and later known throughout the Vancouver music scene as Billy Cowsill's partner, recognized internationally as a great and inspired vocal talent, was also in the car with us, as was bill bissett, founder of the underground blewointment press, and who is now one of Canada's most famous and revered poets and artists.

It was bissett who first spotted and pointed out Dylan sitting in the grey/silver Buick sliding up beside us at the stoplight in the centre lane. "There's Dylan," he yelled, vibrantly excited and delighted. All our faces turned toward the window eagerly. And there the icon was, right beside us.

Two grossly large bearded men wearing garish shirts were in the front seat. Dylan was behind them in the centre of the back seat, sitting upright, prim and alert. We were astonished to see his face so clearly and so close to us. He was sporting a gorgeous Afro permanent like a nimbus around his head, each ash-blonde curl perfectly teased and in place. He looked like a cameo of a hip Victorian dandy, not at all like the ragged and indifferently-dressed beatnik bohemians we were. We expected that, like any normal celebrity, he would nod and smile at us with at least a polite pretense of friendly recognition. Instead, he greeted us with a cold, withering and unmoving stare of disdain.

It was not merely an indifferent snub. It was a frigid look of outright malignant loathing and contempt — as if we were only insects splattered on his windshield. This wasn't Mr. Tambourine Man with his happy wandering Beatle-boot heels that we saw in front of us, but the mystery tramp in "Like a Rolling Stone" gazing at us with the freezing vacuum of his eyes.

To me in that long moment, Dylan appeared as a sick, unhappy goblin. It's been reported since that he was taking a lot of hard drugs in those days, mostly amphetamines, to overcome the exhausting demands of his touring and studio commitments. Exactly during that time, he was in the midst of completing some inspiring but difficult recording sessions in Nashville, assembling his masterpiece double album, *Blonde on Blonde*.

I know that all of us in the car felt stunned and wounded by his attitude. Yet we overcame the moment by quickly inventing the self-assuring consensus that there was nothing the matter with us. The problem was with "Bobby," who was probably feeling sick and unhappy, we decided, forgiving him as we forgave ourselves. He was, after all, we thought, despite being an exalted and brilliant poet hero, like all of us, a single individual in a global movement that was on its way to changing the world.

A few minutes later, Peter Auxier met up with Dylan's companions while buying coffee in the arena before the beginning of the show. "Your boy doesn't look too happy," Peter said to them with his usual disarming candour that was somehow always diplomatic and engaging. As Peter told the story later, Dylan's watchmen responded to him in kind. They were big men, and tough looking, Peter said, and the two of them probably weighed four times as much as the slender Dylan fully dressed and carrying his guitar. They told Auxier that they were being driven crazy with the effort to keep their eye on Dylan every living second. He was looking for a way to break away from them, they said, to escape from the toils of the celebrity that had recently fallen upon him, turning his life into a nightmare of encounters with worshipful stranger fans, so that he no longer recognized either himself or his fans. "There's too much money riding on this guy," they told Peter, "and we can't let him get away from us."

For the record, Dylan took the stage that night like the great professional showman he has always been. He sang a sparkling concert that aroused and enthralled the crowd. He was his normal slightly wry and sarcastic self, but showed no sign at all that he hated his audience and loathed us all like he hated and loathed his own new life as a world-wide celebrity.

A few months later he crashed his motorcycle in upstate New York, and required a long convalescence from his injuries. His own account of the time in the autobiographical *Chronicles, Volume 1*, is complete with a narrative of the harrowing events he underwent as fans descended upon him from everywhere during his attempt to retreat from the public eye. Dylan himself has said that all of his subsequent actions, which included disguises, ruses and identity-change hoaxes of various kinds were needed to break out of his wearying cycle of celebrity and adulation in order to rescue his own personality and his relations with his young family.

In thinking of Dylan's countenance like that of a hateful troll I wondered what might have happened had one of us had a camera and the wit and alacrity to record that shocking envenomed countenance on film.

It has been pointed out many times of late that we live in a world mediated by images, moving and still. It's often said that the collective world view of the public, as much as it can be said to exist, is put together from these same multitudinous images mixed together with words, and that film and photographic images, as presented in the omnipresent modern media, make up a substantial portion of public memory. What would have happened had we somehow found the means to publish that shocking image, with appropriate captions? Would it have changed public perceptions of Bob Dylan as a beloved troubadour genius to display the image of this apparently cold-hearted hateful troll? More likely we would have been blamed for publicising it, besmirching his sainted image, such was the fervour bestowed on Dylan and the Beatles, those other culture heroes of the day. We would have been vilified for revealing that our dreams had been stolen from us by The Man and sold back to us as consumer goods — revolutionary commodities — exposing our counter-culture gods as resting on feet of clay.

Regarding ourselves as self-committed agents of the counter-cultural rebellion, our epiphany of the ultimate chimera of that rebellion put us face to face with the contradictions inherent in the expanding celebrity culture of the globalizing capitalist system of which we had become a part, and the limitations that these relations placed upon even the most exalted of our celebrity icons. We thought that we were equals, brothers and sisters of Bob Dylan within a joint cultural project defined by the solidarity of its actors, but here it was suddenly revealed that we were mere nobodies beside the stars like Dylan and the other cultural heroes created, sustained and promoted in the images of the contemporary media.

Conversely, Dylan had become irretrievably caught up in the dangerous and destructive machinery of this new phase of celebrity culture, felt himself drowning, and blamed us, his fans, for dragging him down, instead of the new media-dominated machinery that he was perhaps as inadvertently complicit in creating as we were.

Because of that new celebrity culture, the current American president was awarded a Nobel Peace Prize even before his election, despite the obvious fact that the United States government has been responsible for more organized violence at home and abroad than any other country in the world. By his own admission, Barack Obama did nothing in the arena of peacemaking to deserve the Nobel award, and now presides over five different armed theatres at various stages of winding up and winding down in parts of the world entirely remote from American home soil.

Pursuing the same vague and undefined outlines of the War on Terror declared by his reactionary predecessor, George W. Bush, Barack Obama, with an academic background in American Constitutional law, brings forward new and ever more menacing security measures in his own country, allowing the American state to peer electronically into the communications of every citizen, undermining the most basic freedoms of the American constitution. A resurgence of the spirit of the 1960s in the form of the Occupy Movement was strangled under his presidency by every legal means available within the American state apparatus at all levels. His government has violated more of its citizens' First Amendment rights than that of all other previous American presidents combined.

The survivors of the sixties protest movements might well now be asking how much their idealism, effort and sacrifice has actually accomplished in terms of effecting positive change over the past half-century.

"Bob Dylan" is a selection from Jamie Reid's Afterword published in *Seize the Time: Vancouver Photographed 1967-1974*, Vladimir Keremidschieff © 2013 New Star Books. Used with permission.

A NIGHT OF NEWLOVE

The Western Front Lodge, the now venerable home of the Vancouver avant-garde art and literary movement of the 1960s and afterwards, was the fitting venue on February 8, 2008 for the launch of a new posthumous selection of the poetry of John Newlove. The launch of this new and definitive selection of his work was accompanied by a remarkable documentary biography of the poet by novice filmmaker Robert McTavish. Newlove was an active presence in the 1960s during the first surge of this local movement of Vancouver art and poetry, along with his now famous and celebrated contemporaries, George Bowering, bill bissett and many others, some of whom appear in the film.

Newlove may not have been positioned exactly in the centre of that fresh and bumptious community, but he was a powerfully influential presence in the near background, along with his circle of friends: the artists Roy Kiyooka, Curt Lang and Fred Douglas; artist-musician Al Neil; and others. Newlove's widow, Susan, is seen commenting in the film about those sometimes disturbing but also exciting days, as poets struggled for their personal and social identities in a new way in new times. Newlove was widely admired by the Vancouver poets and by other poets across the country as the finest poet of his generation.

It would not be quite accurate to say that Newlove was loved by his peers, but he was much admired for his work. People also actually liked him and sought him out for the wit and conversation of his giving moods as much as they feared and avoided his darker moods and unpredictable behaviour. His virtues as a poet and a human being as well as his more than occasional personal charm far outweighed his faults, and people sought him out regardless.

Robert McTavish's insightfully plain and modest film contains a voice-over remark by Shelagh Rogers that by the late 1990s, Newlove was "mainly off the literary map," as he retreated into "alcoholism and solitude." Yet the quality of his work endures through the changes of literary fashion because it speaks to something permanent not only in the Canadian soul alone, but in the modernist sensibility itself. Newlove's work clearly emerges directly and deliberately out of Canadian history and experience.

The event at the Western Front was probably the sign of a deep revival of his lasting reputation. The event was especially remarkable for the quality of its audience, drawn from two generations and from the various notoriously contentious schools of the ongoing Vancouver literary enterprise, people rarely seen together all in one place, including representatives from the highly intellectual postmodernist group of the Kootenay School of Writing and from the more populist performance poets. The variety and difference in the character and style of the attending poets was a sure and complete reflection of the scope of his enduring influence.

Now four years after his death, Newlove's reputation as one of the finest English-language poets of his generation is undergoing this serious revival because his voice obviously continues to speak meaningfully across the generations. Evidence of this is seen in the varied turnout at the event, as well as by the afterword to the new *Selected Poems*, written by Jeff Derksen, a poet and critic of a younger generation, who also made some rather illuminating remarks at the Western Front event.

Robert McTavish's film, *What to Make of it All*, was the unquestionable highlight and delight of the evening. Because of Newlove's actual participation in the film, there can never be a better evocation of his life and work than this remarkable documentary record. This is all the more true because of McTavish's profoundly simple, unpretentious and relatively unvarnished presentation of the life, the poetry and the man. McTavish, a native of Saskatchewan like Newlove, was intrigued by Newlove's work as a student at Simon Fraser University, and the film is the result of his curiosity and deeply sincere concern.

McTavish doesn't shrink in any way from the presentation of Newlove's faults and warts. Simply, but artfully, he places the imperfections of the man alongside the shining perfections of the work and succeeds in creating an all-sided and often touching portrait of the poet and his life. There is a particularly special and revealing moment in the film when Newlove angrily turns upon and actually shouts down his applauding and appreciative audience at one of his final readings in Vancouver. McTavish's creative contribution in the film is to provide in its sound track a repeated diminishing echo of Newlove's own bellowing of "Shut UP!"

As a social person, Newlove could sometimes be uncommonly gracious and generous, but he was also frequently shy and defensive. Often enough, he was moody, unpredictably ornery and difficult... "the glib, obnoxious insulter" as he once described himself. His social manner, as he himself pretends in the film, more than anything else, was a way of seeking attention, or, later, self-contradictorily, a way of keeping people away from him, a reflection of his own self-perceived unloveability. According to his friend, the writer John Metcalf, Newlove was more at home with the "ghostly community of dead poets" than with his living contemporaries.

All these social factors are gracefully brought out in the film, and part of the grace of the film is that it also allows Newlove's great virtues as a poet to stand for themselves, as Newlove himself also would have preferred. Nor does the film suppress the sometimes dark and difficult side of his personality. That dark side in itself is one of the endearing features of his legend in the memory of his friends—cause for much head-shaking and the mood of forgiveness and forebearance for his social sins among them, as gruffly noted by Joe Rosenblatt in his appearance in the film.

Casual and charming, revealing cameo appearances by several contemporaries provide appreciative commentary about the importance of Newlove's work, along with memories of bad and sometimes frightening moments in their personal dealings with him, so often was he consumed with his own self-doubt and even self-contempt.

Douglas Barbour nevertheless remarks that Newlove's work is "something that will stand against that fragmentation." As much as any other Canadian poet of his own post-depression and post-war generation, Newlove lyrically and with understated inner drama, recorded the mood of alienation and fragmentation, of lonesome unbelonging, that many of our generation felt at the time, and that, surely, is part of the reason why his verse continues to survive.

George Bowering avers that there is "so much said there in a language anyone I know can read." Pat Lane: "...an absolutely distinctive verse that he found in himself and on the page." Barry McKinnon speaks of Newlove's great skill and power at compressing the narrative of the most profound emotional moments into poetry. In the midst of a story about Newlove spitting in his face during a long drinking session, Patrick Lane ruefully remarks that Newlove once told him that he "learned one trick" about how to write poetry and that it never failed him, but he never told Lane what it was.

The film provides a treasure trove of such illuminating moments. The great simplicity and modesty of McTavish's documentarist and interview approach somehow magically allows his subjects, including Newlove himself, all the room they need to reveal themselves with full candour. On the way, the film provides some completely new revelations about Newlove's younger life previously hidden away from his friends, and therefore goes a long way towards explaining and even providing some perhaps illusory transparency to some of the enigmas of Newlove's personality and work, especially about the bleakness and the darkness from which his poetry was his main relief and solace.

The film's narrative manages to create a complete biographical form, not entirely tidily, given the messiness of any individual life. It concludes on a relatively happy note, showing Newlove in his final illness following a stroke—surviving decades of personal internal misery and unhappiness, made worse by alcoholism and self-doubt, deliberately resisting fame and applause, yet ultimately arriving during his final illness at a state of relative happiness and welcome self-acceptance.

The illuminating appearances by other poets are interspersed with vignettes from his family life, both as a child amidst the sun and dust of Saskatchewan and as a husband and father in the various cities in which he lived and worked. Susan Newlove and Newlove's stepchildren, Jeremy and Tamsin Gilbert, provide clear-eyed reminiscences about the pain and difficulty of living with his alcoholism and his profound bouts of depression and crippling self-doubt. But they also give testimony to their admiration and affection for him and their great pride in his accomplishment. In spite of himself, Newlove obviously received the affection and admiration of his family and his peers, and not only for his work, but also as a man.

The film presents substantial fragments of his poetry in the form of text moving on the screen, the tapping sound of a typewriter accompanied by Newlove's own deliberately clear, colloquial and unpretentious reading style, enhanced by his compelling voice—the voice of a one-time radio personality. These moments of actual poetry are balanced against Newlove's self-revelatory reflections delivered in his patented, oddly formal manner—plain-spoken, candid, deeply confessional, wry. It seems sometimes as though he is addressing his own ghost or self-image as it exists in the imagination of his contemporaries, or in some ghostly posterity, setting the record straight for himself as much as for others.

Newlove was never a complicated theorist or explainer, preferring that his poetry, the "unyielding phrase," as he once wrote, should stand for itself. Yet there is a very simple moment in the film when he explains with startling clarity his own motive for writing:

"You've got to remember that I AM John Newlove, from Kamsack, and whether I write poems that some people [think] are good, is beside the point. I'm not trying to figure out who I am. That's too silly. I'm just trying to be human, and it takes a long time to learn how."

In the absence of the full biography which still needs to be written, the new *Selected Poems* published by Rob McLennan, and Robert McTavish's fine film, are now the very best and truest places to start to understand Newlove's life and the wellsprings of his art. No university or college library in the country can ever be complete without copies of both the book and the film at hand.

What to Make of it All? The Life and Poetry of John Newlove, directed by Robert McTavish, © 2006 Non-Inferno Media, Moving Images Distribution (http://www.movingimages.ca/catalogue/Art/whattomakeofitall.html)

A Long Continual Argument: The Selected Poems of John Newlove, ed. Robert McTavish, © 2007 Chaudiere Books (http://www.chaudierebooks.com/)

"A Night of Newlove" was previously published in *Pacific Rim Review of Books*, Issue 8, 2008.

ARTIE GOLD

I've been wanting for several days to commemorate the life of Artie Gold, who died a month short of the age of sixty, on Valentine's Day, myself only hearing of it two days ago from his friend Dwight Gardiner, who met Artie in Montreal in the mid-sixties. Artie was a member of the Véhicule group, which included Ken Norris, Stephen Morrissey, Claudia Lapp, John McAuley, Tom Konyves, and Endre Farkas. It was headquartered in the late 1960s at the Yellow Door Coffeehouse near McGill in Montreal, the city where Artie lived all his life, though travelling widely by bus and thumb through the United States according to the normal practice of Canadian poets at the time.

The Véhicule Poets were part of the central Canadian movement of poets influenced by those of the New American Poetry, as well as by the TISH poets from Vancouver, and those gathered around Coach House Press in Toronto. The Véhicule poets are now often said to have been at odds with the older poets of the original Montreal poetry movement and to have taken their inspiration from American models, though their one American-born member, Ken Norris, consistently credits the Montreal native Louis Dudek as his mentor. Artie especially loved the wonderful work of the New York-based Frank O'Hara, for whom he wrote several homages.

I remember the warm hospitality Carol and I received on our arrival in Montreal, both in 1964 and later in 1968 at Artie's home near Pine Avenue, where he lived with a much older woman, Mary Brown, for many years—a warm and intelligent English woman in the mold of Glenda Jackson—and his cats, of which he later wrote that they had ruined his life, and knew it.

He was a small Jewish kid from Montreal, worldly-wise from the outset, and taught me, a Vancouver bumpkin, the sometimes difficult and sophisticated ropes of cosmopolitan Montreal. Although five years younger than I was, he seemed to know so much more about people and life—a very plain-spoken person, and not at all boastful, yet very self-confident and self-possessed. Although he had no significant academic degrees, he was an expert on rocks and plant life, learned through independent study, but rarely spoke of his knowledge.

Once when my partner Carol was in hospital only a day after her second ectopic pregnancy with her life in danger, Artie volunteered to accompany me to see her when I ran into him entirely by chance on the street, myself being in a somewhat desperate state of mind. Carol greeted him with a wan but nevertheless delighted smile, happy to see a friendly face besides my own. His comment in the elevator afterwards: "She's a good soldier, isn't she?" was a canny and welcome observation that gave me courage, too, so I always remember him with gratitude.

Even in his young days, he suffered from the asthma and later the emphysema that finally ended his life, although he kept smoking his unfiltered Pall Malls throughout.

One of the people commenting on the temporary commemoration site set up on the Internet for Artie remarked on his charming smile, visible on the front page of *cityflowers*, published in 1974 by the Presses at Véhicule. That smile, which appeared rarely but always surprisingly on his round, open face, like his poems, spoke of his huge amusement at life, people and the world, but also of a deep affection for it, though sometimes disguised.

My favorites among his poems include this marvel, with its distinctive metaphor of the sea as a snake's belly:

The sea lustrous as a snake's belly
th thousand scales delicately
burning   incandescent   flotsam
of overhead sun   baseball   diamonds
                          by the millions
hinged as seen   overhead from airplanes
approximate scales   little diamonds
approx
              imate

    (and they are milky in texture as the rock
to and fro   as the sea does

    one great quilt beginning in Boston Harbour and
extending to Lisbon
like a net for falling acrobats
                      and
               Icarus's
who lifted by the fact the sun is warm follow it
              its beams, the area
    shone down on

        capturing azures and coppers
      hopelessly on fractional
           canvasses.
                  The sea is not
          exotic
            the sea
      is mediterranean
        middle
    of the earth   the sea
        is birth
    the sea is the floating gestures
branches on it make, rocking
              to and fro
      with green berries
      and wood splinters
                  of men who
  desire passage   at certain speeds

the sea is   interrupted life of liquid gold

                  (th dark blues and azures
    are man's
anticipation

THE BICYCLE, THE RADIO, AND THE LOWLY SLUG: THE POETRY OF GERRY GILBERT

Vancouver's at-the-post modernist poet, Gerry Gilbert, published his first collection of verse thirty years ago. It was named *White Lunch*, after a legendary string of cafeterias located since time immemorial down Granville from Robson and along Hastings Street almost to Main. In its heyday, the White Lunch was just that—racist. But by the 1950s it was a place where the poor and unemployed who occupied the surrounding fleabag hotels in Vancouver's precious stretch of North American downtown could find a cheap, hot, nutritious meal: porridge, soup, bread, stew. Not fast food, and definitely not in a hurry. Gilbert's writing is like that—it fills a need, it's there when it's required.

For many recent years, Gilbert lived in a tiny two-story cottage not much larger than a child's play house sequestered in the lane behind a Powell Street restaurant, half a block from Oppenheimer Park in Vancouver's Downtown East Side. The area certainly qualifies as a major spiritual centre of the city—a refuge for the poor, the crippled, the homeless, the despised, the broken, the alcoholic and the drug-addicted. The area is also the centre of Vancouver's polyglot population of Chinese, Japanese, East Indian, French, Slavic and Aboriginal peoples. Whatever else the neighbourhood might be, with its very real and present dangers of heroin, cocaine and murder, it is certainly the underbelly of the city, one of the places where the huge social gap between the rich and the poor of Vancouver is all too painfully visible.

In physical appearance, Gilbert is not much different from the people he lives among. He looks like a throw-back to an earlier kind of Canadian, the kind you see in black and white and sepia photographs of the 1930s and 1940s—wry, wiry, underfed, perhaps consumptive with a red dot of color on the upper part of a bony cheek beneath the slightly-cocked eye of a sharply-seeing bird, dressed in cinder grey with a jaunty cap atop his bony Scottish, blue-eyed face, modest and diffident, yet confident and even spirited, like a railway-man, a skinny and diminutive seaman, a poor clergyman in a poor neighbourhood—canny and quick. Up close, there is a surprising, bony, physical substantiality about him. Farther away, he appears more insubstantial, seems to blend unobtrusively into the crowd and the background. When he dons his white helmet and lifts his bones onto his bicycle, he looks like someone's ghost about to deliver an important message from the world beyond.

Gilbert is legendary among the other poets of the city as the poet who rides a bicycle, a kind of Hermes on two wheels. Like the hermaphroditic, androgynous Greek messenger god, the silver-tongued patron of poets, thieves and con-men, the fluid and changeable divinity who carries the news between the gods of Olympus, and between the gods and humans, Gilbert rides swiftly between poetry readings, which he records on tape and later broadcasts on his radio program every Sunday evening and every second Thursday afternoon on Vancouver Co-op Radio, where he comments with his subtle diplomacy, his silver Hermes tongue on the local literary, artistic and political scene.

A Vancouverite of the 1960s vintage to his bones, Gilbert's politics are socialist, his religion is Buddhist of the Zen variety, his poetics and his metaphysics resolutely modernist and avant garde. He is as much at home with the literary techniques of Joyce and Stein as with the conceptual relativism and indeterminacy of Einstein and Heisenberg. His entry into literary modernism was precipitated by the beat generation, by Henry Miller, Jack Kerouac and William Burroughs, but in the course of his writing career, he has assimilated the inner lessons of all the main trends of artistic modernism, from Dada to post-pop, converting what was useful to him into part of his own distinctive aesthetic approach, which has always been at the leading edge of Canadian literary production. He was a language poet before there was such a thing as "language poetry."

Sometime in the late 1960s, Gilbert made the decision to frame his life, work and social contribution within the civic ambience of the city of Vancouver, because, he says, he likes the drip-drip-drip of the rain. Gilbert locates his work within a collective literary and artistic enterprise launched in Vancouver in the late 1950s and early 1960s—a movement sometimes referred to as the "downtown poets," so as to set them apart from the poets of TISH and other poets more closely connected to the universities. The so-called "downtown poets" include diverse talents like Al Neil, bill bissett, Fred Douglas, Roy Kiyooka, and two unduly neglected women poets, Judith Copithorne and Maxine Gadd, all of whom Gilbert credits with having influenced his work in some way. In one way or another, all of these artists reflect a broader artistic concern than the merely literary, and have involved themselves in other fields of artistic production, including the visual arts and performance art. And in one way or another, all of these artists, despite the universality of their concerns, locate their work within the specific local context of Vancouver and the West Coast.

With typical quirky humour, Gilbert has chosen as his personal totem the slow and lowly garden slug: green, slime-covered, hermaphrodite, nocturnal, the most typical fauna of the Vancouver rain forest. What's more real than a slug? Images of the slug appear throughout his poetry, along with a calligram, which Gilbert invented and which has become his secret logo.

"I've got a sense of history, and here's some good advice: the only material you can make history of is *honesty*. Honesty is judging in terms of space, and not the other way around. The other way around, time (the money, the lie, the makeup) is the death of space. What I get from next spring is the distance. Because like the slug, I'm always right there. In the way. On the way. Speed for me is how far I can see. From here. You should see me really go. Honestly." ("The Slug," *From Next Spring*, p. 188.)

Gilbert has certainly always been there when it counted, ready to go the distance as he says. As a matter of conscious policy, he has upheld ancient poetic traditions, which assign the poet in the community a role as scribe, recorder, chronicler and historian. Steady activity through three decades has made Gilbert one of the most prolific archivists, chroniclers and recorders of poetic activity in Vancouver. His *radiofreerainforest* program has probably provided an outlet for more local and national writers than any other medium, printed, aural or visual in the entire country.

Gilbert's own poetic and imaginative output has also been immense, given the poverty of the means that have been made available to him. Since the appearance of *White Lunch* in 1964, he has produced a stream of chapbooks, books, pamphlets, magazines, and broadsheets. An incomplete bibliography drawn from a curriculum vitae prepared by Gilbert himself lists twenty-four titles, each representing a complete and self-contained collection of writing and poetry, published by a wide and far-flung variety of legendary avant-garde publishers: bill bisset's blewointment press, the *Georgia Straight Writing Supplement,* Talonbooks of Vancouver, Coach House Press of Toronto, Weed/Flower Press, grOnk, etc. For many years, he has also singlehandedly edited and published his own magazine, *B.C. Poetry Monthly.*

The titles of his books include *Skies* (Talonbooks, 1974); *Grounds* (Talonbooks, 1976); *From Next Spring* (Coach House Press, 1977); *Moby Jane* (Coach House Press, 1986); and his most recent collection, *Azure Blues* (Talonbooks, 1991). There are besides, more than a dozen small monographs, published and self-published in a variety of formats.

Literary work is only a portion of Gilbert's overall artistic activity. At one time or another he has worked in film, video, photography, drama, and various forms of performance art combining poetry, dance, music, and visual media. He laments that his lack of money prevents him from doing more work these days in photography.

During the course of his career, he has collaborated on projects of varied kinds with practically every well-known Vancouver writer, as well as hundreds of less well-known writers and artists. He has appeared on the same stage with internationally-known writers and artists like Robert Creeley, Allan Ginsberg, John Weiners, Yvgeny Yevtushenko, John Cage, Anne Waldman, Robert Duncan, Tom Pickard, Margaret Atwood and John Newlove.

His name, along with the names of many other ignored and forgotten Vancouver artists, appears frequently in the catalogue of the activities at the Vancouver Art Gallery during the 1960s and 1970s, the days of the seminal activities of Intermedia, when the gallery was a real staging place for the activities of the locally-rooted *avant-garde*.

The activities of the 1960s and the 1970s were the launching pad of the active Vancouver artists today, in the sense that the artists and writers of the 1960s and the 1970s first organized and mobilized the core of the broad audience that patronises literary and artistic modernism in Vancouver today. Gilbert gives this account:

"When I came back here in the early 60s [from Britain], the circles of friends were accumulating, & by the middle 60s enough people knew each other to make things in the city happen — I bet it was the biggest local cultural bloom that had ever happened in English Canada, & it's grown & seeded since then." ("Outerview," *Grounds*, no page numbers.)

But when the rewards and applause were handed out, Gilbert was passed over and ignored, though there is hardly a poet writing in B.C. today who does not recognize Gilbert as a master. In my knowledge, some of Canada's finest poets, including Michael Ondaatje, George Bowering, Victor Coleman, Barry McKinnon, are all avid admirers of Gerry Gilbert's work. Yet these days Gilbert cannot get a grant to save his life.

Gilbert's activity has been offered to the city and the country freely, without hope or expectation of recognition or reward. It is easy to say that when you demand no reward, you don't get any, and Gilbert has certainly never demanded any reward.

Gilbert consequently lives on welfare today. He is barely

able to scrape his rent together every month, he's often out "hunting the wild tofu" at the end of the month, and is helpless to do anything about the decay of his teeth. His recent writing provides a steady record of his dental history—not because Gilbert is egotistical, complaining or mournful. He cheerfully regards the state of his own body as one clear index of the state of the economy and the nation. He knows that if he is suffering, others are suffering worse. Yet he keeps on producing poetry and giving his support to all the writers of the city, old and new, because that, in his view, is what needs to be done.

In this respect, he is like a Buddhist monk: the vow of poverty is the basis of his spiritual freedom. Gilbert sustains his life and makes his poetry out of the most narrowed and restricted means.

It is difficult to say whether choice or compulsion governs these realities. Would Gilbert's work change if his economic circumstances suddenly improved? Gilbert himself says that he is holding out to be paid for his poetry. "It's what I do," he says, "To make a living at anything else would undermine the credibility of the art."

Gilbert's statement can be interpreted from a variety of different perspectives. From the perspective of some other poets who make their living by teaching in the academies, the statement implies a criticism about the credibility of their art. One thing is certain: Gilbert would not be at home in the atmosphere of the universities, any more than the poets who work from the academies would find themselves at home in the place where Gilbert lives.

Gilbert's life gives existential credibility to his work. It is an act of courage and resistance merely to keep working at all in the conditions under which Gilbert lives. In crazy circumstances, Gilbert keeps his humour sane:

"You're sitting too far forward, too far over, and it doesn't matter which way tips, you fall off and the vines catch around the edges of flatness and grow you a whole new moment to live to forget as if you weren't already in always enough hot water for a shower of housework, the cabin clean enough to read; don't and it gets dirty again, 'don't look down,' you always say, of what you want, a floor, 'leave your shoes on but wash your hands, lean into your level best, keep it as clean as you can reach.'"

"Revise tomorrow into the second person. We're not being paid to be happy. We just can't help it. Paper and pencil out to a stretch away in every room: studio, kitchen, study, toilet, dipper little. Pads, little loose-leaf notebooks, bound but undated diaries, odd-sized slips cut from the blanks of rejected versions; nothing that will fit in the typewriter; so the cat on the couch falls asleep waiting for someone to get to work on that irritable idea of an itch between his ears." (untitled prose poem from *PER*, p. 9.)

It's all there, including everything that's not there, the space that isn't there in the cramped quarters, the food that has already been eaten, the money that isn't there to replace it, the time available that ought to be plentiful but isn't, because in order to be able to work, one must first prepare by cleaning up and clearing the space, all the details of living in poverty that can easily obstruct the creative act, and yet it is the creative act that makes it all possible and livable: "We're not being paid to be happy. We just can't help it."

Gilbert's recent work is centred around a new book called PERHAPS. The book is conceived as a three-part project. The first part covers last year in the cottage behind Powell Street, and is called PURR; the second covers the first year in his Strathcona shack, and is entitled PER; the third, called HAPS, covers the second year there and is not completed yet. Up to now the writing runs to more than 100 single-spaced pages — almost a page a week. His application this year to the Canada Council for funds to complete the book was rejected for the third time. Gilbert continues to work on the book notwithstanding.

Gilbert's agenda and approach have not changed since he began to be a poet thirty years ago:

"Poetry is an evolving language," he says, "constantly giving each language back to the place—like the tribe or class of people—it came from. I test language." ("Outerview," *Grounds*, no page numbers).

He is interested to know not only what language can do, but what it can't do, too:

"I'm interested in the syntax, the housekeeping. The language is ours. Poets garden it, keep it new, which is ancient. Formally, that's sort of what I'm doing. The words on the page, the people on the place. Or, I'm writing my life story as it keeps happening. A myth—a perfectly ordinary story & notably so, because it's hard to notate & not get all twisted into the letters."

For Gilbert, poetry is part of an on-going collective enterprise, an activity that he shares with other poets and artists, past and present, and with his living readership.

Gilbert's unique relationship to his readership is what sets him apart from all other contemporary poets in Canada. His fully avant-garde character lies in the fact that his writing makes almost no concession to conventional notions of what writing should be, what writing should do. Whatever others may think that writing should do, Gilbert thinks and demands that it should do something else.

His first aesthetic principle is that writing should be "completely free of all artistic ambition." "Any other attitude," Gilbert contends, "taints the artistic process."

Artistic ambition taints the artistic process; true art requires the absence of artistic ambition—Gilbert is expert at balancing such apparently contradictory statements, which are really not self-contradictory, but subtly dialectical. The principle itself is one that he adopted from "the craftspeople," in particular, from the legendary British potter, Bernard Leach, with whom Gilbert worked and studied informally in Cornwall during the late 1950s.

According to Gilbert, poets and potters alike sustain a sacramental relationship with their materials: the potter with the earth from which the pot is made; the poet with the words from which the poem is made. "This is the material of the universe," Gilbert says, implying that the best and most useful poetry is made of the simplest coos and grunts, just as the best and most useful pots are made of simple clay.

Consistent with this basic principle, Gilbert deliberately avoids the verbal pyrotechnics, the fancy word play, the rich, seductive use of words, images and metaphor conventionally understood as "poetic language." Most typically he writes in the barest monosyllables: two-syllable words are rare in Gilbert, three-syllable words almost non-existent. In this sense, he is a minimalist poet, restricting his palette to the barest necessities, extracting the widest possible meanings from the simplest possible means.

In the "real" world of commerce and exchange, in the media, in advertising and in politics, words are typically used to impose meaning by swamping it, to deceive, to manipulate, to bully, to overwhelm and to coerce: in a word, to sell. Gilbert subversively reduces the scale of the communicative process, cuts it down to human size. He conspires somehow to look his reader directly in the eyes, to invite the reader to dance with him. His music is the plain insistent music of the coffee-spoon in the kitchen, of the man who hums to himself while he goes about the simple tasks of the day. These human activities go on everywhere despite the size and noise of the world outside. Yet Gilbert says he's always ready to take his poetry to a larger space. "It fills the space it's in," he says. "If the space is bigger, you just have to make it louder."

Gilbert is not opposed to technological and social progress; he merely refuses to worship at its altar, demanding that technology serve the cause of human freedom rather than the aims of power and profit:

"It's their sense of time & power equals speed that I'm trying to derail...and that's not some crazy weird stoned reflex of mine, it's my view of myself in the situation, I keep looking so I won't vanish into the tube. They are scared to look which is scary, that the people who claim to own the world are running on fear. Be brave me hearties! Let me show you what fear is! Watch me dance!" ("The Slug," *From Next Spring*, pp. 187-188.)

Thus, for Gilbert, poetry is not a special, privileged activity, but a normal one, like breathing, like walking, like talking. Artistic ambition, the desire to make something "special," a privileged "art object," is alien to the process of real creation and to the person-to-person connections which creation is supposed to engender.

"The poem is not the eager heroism or the dismal gloom of the job all day…what poem!? This writing? Well, it isn't 'made for tv.' There's no particular 'desired effect.' The poem is the food itself, it isn't the leftovers, the shit. It's made for You. Once." (*From Next Spring*, p. 177)

Poetry, Gilbert says, is nothing special. It is merely something vital. It is food. Gilbert creates poetry not so much to create something beautiful as to point out what is merely recognizable, familiar, present.

Living as he does in straitened circumstances and in small quarters, Gilbert's world is at once smaller and larger than the world of most other Canadian poets. He is forced to make poetry out of the pittance that remains to him: hence, cats, flies, fleas, spiders, mice, slugs, lint, snot, farts, hair, fungus, dishes, dirt and all the other details of daily living find their way into his poems.

These ordinary things are not in the least made extraordinary by having become the subject matter of poetry. On the contrary, they merely seem to become more what they truly are. And this is the magic of Gilbert's verse: what is usually passed over, ignored, dismissed and discarded, suddenly appears in all its plain reality, with all its bald, irreducible existential truth.

"I don't look like myself, but my place looks like me. 'I'm just camping here,' I always say, to explain why the walls aren't painted, the floor not washed, the plumbing hand held. I'll be myself in a couple of days when the laundry, the vacuuming, the shopping, a bath, give me back. Then I'll look like myself.

Does your place look like you? Do you look like your face? 'Only when you look,' I always say. The faster the fish, the wetter the pond.

I've tried all variations & combinations of moustache, beard, hair & smile, & never looked like me; so I tried not trying, & not trying not trying, & I never even looked, which is not like me. So while you're here, I'll jut look like you, if you like. The boulder, the fish, the water, the pond.

I take a quick drink of cold snap tap water from the tap to rinse my mouth out & feel the size of my mouth. Look out. The deeper the fish, the taller the pond." (from the bookmark to *Moby Jane*)

Here you have a short record of the struggle of a living person to create a private identity and a public face out of the ordinary objects that surround him. Everything is completely plain and unadorned—yet there is real magic here, real transformative power. The changing syntax and construction of the final sentence of each paragraph points to a complex, shifting engagement between the writer and his interlocutor (the "you" of the poem), between the things which occupy his life and the way he sees them, internalizes them, makes them part of himself.

Long ago, Gerry Gilbert wrote a poem in which he quoted the diary of a Vietnamese NLF guerilla, conflating the activities of the guerilla, the "men stepping out of space capsules," and the first steps of an infant daughter. "MY DAYS AND TASKS BELONG TO HISTORY," he wrote in capital letters, as if to emphasize that bloody wars, space travel and normal daily activities co-exist in the same world. He concluded:

> We will never diminish
> I will die first
>
> Look! the tortured Guerilla's face has no skin!
> & he has not betrayed you

You are not alone
You have survived

Days, Tasks, Belong to History

Say yes, yes

YOUR BABY BELIEVES YOU

("Space Poem," *New Wave Canada*, Contact Press, Toronto, 1966, editor Raymond Souster, p. 51.)

Gilbert has sustained this credo throughout thirty years of work: the human world is made up of the simplest materials. What is essential is not the power of the means that are used, but the power of the nexus of fellow-feeling between human beings. When that is gone, only noise, power and speed remain.

Nevertheless, in Gilbert's world, objects and their names, or rather the unity the two of them make together, sustain a kind of mastery over the human. Owing to the fact that objects are NAMED objects, they become symbols. These symbols take on a life of their own, a life which is both dependent on the material objects and independent of them. The interaction between objects and language, between things and their names, transforms both: they become protean beyond their natural changeableness. They become objects of culture, of thought, of human art. Artefacts become naturalized and objects become artefacts, human constructs.

In a certain sense, the objects of sense ARE the human, because the human cannot constitute itself without them, without the objects and their names. Without his hat, without his bicycle, without his cats, without his typewriter, without the paper on which his poems are typed, without the slugs that come and go within his poems, without his friends to inhabit and to hear the poems, where is Gerry Gilbert?

So it is a human world that Gilbert celebrates. In this world, the human is not seen or represented as naturally aggressive and acquisitive. Rather, with Gilbert, it is the social and co-operative side of human existence that counts the most. Gilbert asks only for what he truly needs, he lives and lets live, he acts as a poet with collective aims in mind.

Surrendering to the social need is not an intellectual activity for Gilbert, not a mere philosophical conclusion. It is a necessity imposed by the practical realities of his life. The reality that Gilbert strives to build does not flow from an abstract ideological principle. It flows from the reality that he actually, truly, daily, lives.

THE LEGACY OF WARREN TALLMAN

Warren Tallman, who died on the 1st of July, 1994 and thereby achieved his final independence, has now become history. That is, he has become something other than he actually was in the flesh. He has become a construction, an idea, a fiction, no longer a real person, his identity while alive now sunk in various representations, none of them capable of fully embracing the richness and variety of the whole personality. Historical and critical commentaries on the life and work of Warren Tallman can never be anything else but constructions, or reconstructions, refittings and retoolings of the facts and the narrative into a format recognizable within the current social, political, economic and literary environment. In these new contexts, Warren becomes by the natural process of history and change, something other than he was in the flesh. The entire personality that Warren was disappears into a set of ideas and abstractions, his body disappears, his weaknesses, his booze, his cigarettes, his bursts of temper, everything in short that made him into a living human being, a companion who lived amongst us, *In the Midst*.

Yet it is important for all of us to remember the past, to create history, and to recreate history, to take from memory, recorded or otherwise, what the present requires, so I am bound to do the same.

The most important thing that can be said at this moment about the personality of Warren Tallman is that this entire event in which we are today participating would not be taking place at all if it had not been for the life and work of Warren Tallman, because without Warren there would have been no TISH, and without TISH, this series of talks and discussions would not be taking place at all. This is not to say that TISH and these events depended then or now only and solely on Warren Tallman and Warren Tallman's vision and activity. Warren's role, besides the example that he gave to us, was an enabling role, and by his activity he empowered a group of individuals, each of whom were strong personalities in their own right, with a strong drive toward self-actualization, toward making concrete achievements in the real world of literary production.

In the atmosphere of the late 1950s and early 1960s before TISH was born, we were so used to the idea that nothing of any importance ever happened in Vancouver, that my friend Peter Cameron was excited beyond words to tell me that the author of an article in Evergreen Review about Jack Kerouac whose writing had aroused us so profoundly, was actually a professor at UBC, living right here in our very own city. Peter, who came from an intellectual background had no sense of shyness about approaching this exalted personage, looking him up at his office and later reporting to me that this author, far from being hip and cool in the style of the time, was instead a skinny and nervous cigarette addict whose fingers were stained with nicotine and who shook throughout his entire body as he lit one cigarette after another, sometimes leaving the last one still burning in the overflowing ashtray on his desk. But there was also about him an air of restless intellectual energy and the nervousness was part of this energy. Later, I too met him in the hall and went with Peter to his office where we discussed what we had been reading, the magazines, Jack Kerouac, Ginsberg, Norman Mailer, the writers in the campus newspaper and the campus literary magazine, who included George Bowering, Mike Mathews and Maxine Gadd, who are still around today. This professor spoke to me not quite like an equal, but almost so, as though he had a kind of knowledge and some mastery which he wished to share and which required my approval in a way that the pronouncements of no other teacher that I had ever met so far ever seemed to do.

Vancouver today has become a city of poets and of poetry, officially underappreciated as they surely are. Today in Vancouver, (within the city itself, not including the academies), there are at least four venues where poetry is regularly read and appreciated. I doubt that this number can be matched by any other city of comparable size in the English-speaking world. As we commemorate again today the life of Warren Tallman, many of us remember a time in the history of the city when there was only one such venue, and that venue was centred around the home of Warren and Ellen Tallman.

There are other comparable figures in the history of Vancouver literature: Earle Birney is one, and George Woodcock is another, but they belong to another era and another style. Warren Tallman, more than any other single individual, represents the birth of Vancouver poetic modernism, latterly called post-modernism—he is the evangelist, the father of Vancouver literary modernism, and his children are numerous, although many of them may not even know his name.

The children of every father sustain a mixed, ambiguous relation with their progenitor. They are aware, more than others outside the family relationship, of the human flesh and blood character of their parent, of his weaknesses, rather than of his strengths. Sometimes, children fear their fathers, but this is the last relationship that anyone could ever have had with Warren. What stands out and is remembered about his character is his sometimes maddening helplessness, his inability to bring any kind of matter to any kind of satisfactory conclusion. No sooner are things begun under his hand, it seems, than they begin to take on dimensions which in their vast uncertainties, he himself no longer can control. This is as true of his teaching method as it is of his writing and his organizing efforts. Yet all of us have gained by it, by this very weakness, which has forced us time and again to take the initiative and to follow through from Warren's glittering beginnings to the most unexpected of conclusions. Because the new in life and in the world often appears in the guise of the chaotic, the confused, and confusion, not only to the defenders of the old order, but also to the actual participants in change, the acceptance and recognition of Chaos is the most important insight for any contemporary poet, and Warren has been just the man to bring this recognition to abundant life. Through Warren, a whole generation of Vancouver poets was allowed to sustain a nourishing relationship with Chaos.

It was through the activities of Warren Tallman that the writers and the literary community of Vancouver were brought into contact with the wider world outside the old parochial Canada and the latter day frontier city, which Vancouver was in those days. Some people in the past have created an imaginary "Canadian poetic tradition," which Warren Tallman, the American, allegedly disrupted, acting even, some suggested, as the agent of the CIA, of American cultural imperialism.

How strange and ridiculous these charges seem today in the light of the fact that Canadians are still confronted with a massive U.S. cultural aggression and imperialism, while what Warren has helped to bring to light in reality acts as a bulwark against that flood of Disneyism combined with the culture of spectacular violence. By giving us access to the best and the most critical of the American tradition, Warren has helped us to possess our own imaginations. No people in the present world can possess their own imaginations without reference to a larger world, and that larger world, for Canadians, must always and above all, include Americans—geography and history determine this reality and it cannot be evaded.

None of this has any meaning outside at least some discussion of the prevailing political and cultural atmosphere in the world at large as it affected our own lives in this city in the early 1960s. North America was barely emerging from the fog and repression of McCarthyism in the darkest and coldest early days of the Cold War, correctly characterized in later days as a North American form of fascism. The liberal democracy in the United States was still in the process of overcoming this fear-ridden, paranoid political and social psychosis, the influence of which has still not been purged from the North American environment and still strives for a resurgence in the circumstances under which we currently live, in which the President of the United States has declared that all those who do not support the measures which the American State has unilaterally decided are the means of "America's New War" on international terrorism, is on the side of the terrorists.

In the meantime (speaking again of the early 1960s), the highest levels of the American state, in the name of fighting communism, had sanctioned every kind of terrorist activity against all who dared to resist and to demand that the freedoms of actual life in the American democracy should live up to the rhetoric of its leaders. The North American state sanctioned massive violence around the world and within the very borders of the United States itself, to the extent that the police and other armed agents of the various levels of the state, felt perfectly justified and even secure from punishment in murdering young people in the south who fought for the right of Afro-Americans to exercise that most fundamental of all democratic rights, the right to vote. If it had not been for the vast movement of the American people, these criminals would never have been brought to justice at all, as some of them finally were, many years later.

The years of the early, middle and late 1960s were filled with the news of wars and assassinations: Malcolm X, John F. Kennedy, Martin Luther King, to name only a few of the more well-known assassinations in the American body politic. And these were accompanied by events threatening the outbreak of a world holocaust in the form of nuclear war: The Bay of Pigs invasion, the Cuban missile crisis, the war in Vietnam.

The howls of the Beat Generation, which many of us young people heard in those days, were only one voice, one node, one nexus, one gathering site though one of the first of the many voices which became part of the widespread resistance of the North American population, a resistance which grew and became more widespread in the middle and later sixties, burgeoning into a movement which changed the surface of the racial landscape in the United States, and finally played an important though not decisive role in the humiliating defeat which the U.S. war machine suffered on the battlefields of Vietnam after killing 2 million of the Vietnamese people. I have said that the surface of the racial landscape changed, because the depths remain the same. In the middle sixties, while the American government waged a failing war on soil half way around the world from their home territory, America itself writhed internally with a kind of war, as the black ghettoes of the major cities of America exploded with the too-long contained rage and outrage of the trampled Afro-American minority. The decade ended with an orgy of state violence against the dissidents: seventeen leaders of the Black Panther party were killed in their homes and on the streets by armed agents of the state, the FBI and local law enforcement officers acting against what J. Edgar Hoover called "the greatest threat to America's internal security," while at the same time, the National Guard at Kent State opened fire on dissenting students, killing four of them and arousing even wider doubt and opposition in the American population in the process.

These events were a kind of culmination to what might be called the fulmination that was gathering in the early sixties when Warren Tallman presided over the discussion sessions that gave rise to TISH. At UBC in the early 1960s, there was a strong contingent of American professors that had refused to take the loyalty oath to the United States imposed by the McCarthyites who had scored a virtual, though temporary *coup d'état* with their political creation, the House Un-American Activities Committee, through which they worked night and day to criminalize and persecute every kind of political dissent. Though I rarely discussed politics with Warren, I somehow assumed that he was part of that movement, even though he had no direct connection with the actual group of protesting professors. An anarchist by political conviction, although in my view probably a naive one, he pointed to the example of Black Mountain College as the model of the kind of school required to sponsor the kind of art and literature which our times required.

The rantings of Canadian chauvinism are based on the false premise that Americans, as people, are capable of nothing good. This is easy enough to believe, given the aggressiveness and vacuity of conventional American cultural products. But Americans, too, suffer from this problem, perhaps more than anybody else. And hence there is resistance in the U.S.A. itself to these aggressively dominant forms of corporate culture, which work against the human and national spirit of others. There was and is resistance. And to my mind, Warren Tallman and the poets he brought to Canada represent part of that trend of resistance.

During the Gulf War, for example, Allen Ginsberg appeared on American television for the first time in my memory in twenty years, to deliver a stinging Jeremiad against the American war activities as something inconsistent with all the ideals on which the American republic is supposedly founded. Throughout all of those terrifying events, Ginsberg was the only American public figure that I observed on television who had the courage to speak out so decisively against that American war.

Warren Tallman and Ellen Tallman, as much as any other two human beings, were responsible for bringing Canadians into living contact with this brave American poet.

To be a teacher of poets, as Warren Tallman was, one must be at least half a poet oneself, and Warren was more than half a poet. No poet today can live in harmony with the existing order of the world: a poet must be at least in some sense the enemy of order, whether of the old or the new variety. In the early days of what we sometimes liked to call the Vancouver poetry renaissance, Warren was fond of quoting Plato, that ancient reactionary and enemy of poetry, who was forever expressing his fear that a new music could shake the walls of the city. In opposition to Plato and the entire camp of order, Warren above all fought for the hegemony of the new music, not the old. He and Ellen provided us with a venue for the expression of our young, chaotic energies. But more than this, he provided us with the beginnings of a theory, and a method. None of the former TISH poets may practice this theory in the form that it was given to us then, but all of us, I am sure, are rooted in the foundation that he laid down. I am merely going to read a few quotes from his essays published in *Godawful Streets of Man* to illustrate the importance that he ascribed to the human attachment to language and its rhythms as the basis of a new verse, a new music:

From *Kerouac's Sound*
"...this dual progression in which the syncopated beat of the melody escalator carries the spontaneous action of the improvisations from level to level has given way, with the advent of Bop, to a music which seems to travel from level to level on the improvisations alone. That is, the melody (the escalator) has been assimilated into the pattern of improvisations (hop, skip, jump) and the improvisations—always the life impulse of jazz—have determined this merger. At best, Bop has freed jazz from the tedium of banal melodies. It has also given emphasis to a principle of spontaneous creative freedom which has been taken over by the Beat writers in ways likely to have a strong influence upon North American poetry and fiction."

From *Mad Song: Allen Ginsberg's San Francisco Poems*
"The field of words stands as a centuries-long culling from the nature of things of the whole sum of our general intelligence, a word universe corresponding to our universe. The great advantage of the universe of words consists in its flexible plasticity and reach in contrast to the rigidity, lumpishness and confinement of our city street field. But the great danger of this advantage is that same freedom which prompts poets to seek out crucial corners where all that is extraordinary about man is located, and the disadvantage of such corners is that in the human universe they are likely to be abysses of heights where that single intelligence which maintains the integrity of the universe is most likely to grow dizzy or disunited. Hence the need for an apprenticeship in a mechanics which will maintain this integrity of the whole those times the poet's perceptions carry him to corners where he comes upon otherwise unsupportable dimensions of the human."

From The Eternal Mood: Robert Duncan's Devotion to Language
"As his life in poetry unfolds he assimilates innovations of all the important Modernists—Pound, T.S. Eliot, Gertrude Stein, WC Williams, HD, Hart Crane, Louis Zukofsky, Charles Olson... Duncan's poetry testifies to a constantly growing and deepening belief, derived most directly from Ezra Pound, in the supreme importance, the reality of language. Language as he understands it is at once the raw material and the natural habitat of poetry, a kind of universe that is subject to the same laws and opportunities as the human, natural and supernatural worlds."

In *Proprioception in Charles Olson's Poetry*, representing Charles Olson as the inheritor of Ezra Pound's pioneer activities examining the resources of language as Cezanne is said to have examined the resources of paint as the foundation of his own efforts to found a modernist art, Warren writes:
"'Projective Verse' is a first blueprint for a unified movement in language of the poet's full intelligence as Olson names the parts and puts them together into a working model. His vehicle is speech, language from the mouth. The energies that Pound discerned are distributed and synchronized as intellect moves 'over' by way of the syllable, monitored by the ear, and emotion moves 'under' by way of the heart, the beat beat beat."

Negotiating the aporias, the chasms of triumphant North American individualism and the relation of the living human individual to living nature, Warren writes in relation to Charles Olson's notions of proprioception:
"Each of us is single, separate, apart—inside our skins. But by breaking through to proprioception, 'sensibility within the organism by movement of its own tissues,' he discovers an individuality of the organism itself, a physical being that precedes spiritual, social or psychological being. Flesh first, and from the flesh a bodying forth of the soul, self, or ego. His advice to persons who were extended beyond themselves was often simply 'go home.' For him the home was the body in which we dwell, our eyes are home, our ears, our intellects, emotions—a human house."

Within this human house, the poets of Vancouver are still marginalized today, as we were then, but there are many more of us, and our voice is louder. The walls of the city are already shaking at least slightly, and this is owing, in large measure, to the unrelenting activities of Warren Tallman from the l960s through the 1980s to bring poetry to its audience, to make poetry part of the living fabric of our city.

Warren's greatest strength as a teacher was his preference for live poets (indeed live people) over dead ones, and this strength put him in opposition to the gentlemen of the academy, the English Departments, the Philosophy Departments etc., whose role too often is to enshrine and to embalm the dead, to canonize them, to ensure, above all, that they are truly dead and can exercise no serious influence on the lives of the living.

As a human being, Warren was extraordinarily close to all of his students, and he had a particular ability to locate and encourage the unique talents of particular individuals. He could bring out things that no other teacher could. Apart from that, every resource of his life was available to his beloved poets all the time. There was nothing he would refuse to a poet in need—his house, his car, his money, his reputation, everything that he possessed was freely given to any of us who needed it. There are legendary examples of this incredible generosity. They probably thought he was a fool.

My other image of Warren is the image of the night at the Mingus concert at the Cellar (circa 1962), where skinny, frail Warren, all elbows, knees and splayed fingers, interposed himself between the raging, smoldering hulk of Charles Mingus and a local football player, a graduate of my own high school, whom Mingus had a second before, walloped with a bathroom plunger for continuing to mock his demands for respectful quiet for the band's music. In retrospect, it seems to me that Mingus was the representative of the nascent forces of the civil rights movement in the United States. One of the towering geniuses of jazz, he has never been given credit for his most important innovation: not Henry Mancini, not even

Quincy Jones, is the inventor of television jazz. That honour goes to Charles Mingus, as the original liner notes written by Mingus for *Ah Um*, decisively prove. That night, the giant bassist and his band were playing the angry, aggressively satirical Mingus composition: "Fables of Faubus," recalling the racist Alabama governor who had refused to allow black students to attend white schools. The composition was accompanied with a galvanizing and shocking chant: Faaaaw buus, Faaaawbus, Nazi, Fascist, Suprematist. My classmate football hero, witlessly became the instrument of white America and its racism, its disregard for all that black America and other races of the world have contributed to civilization. The peculiar thing about that evening, is that I experienced no conflict of loyalties. Even though I was a pacifist by conviction in those days, I was totally on Mingus' side.

The football player threw a careless right at Mingus' head, which Mingus caught on the fly in his ham fist and with a flick of his wrist, flung the football player like a frisbee across three tables, and then turned to perhaps finish the job as the football player struggled to gain his feet and balance. The fight would not have ended, had not Warren, looking like a tiny vulnerable spider who had dropped from the ceiling, interposed himself twitching and gesticulating between the two behemoths. With his arms crossed in an X and his fingers spread and waving, Warren called out in his sharp professor's voice "Charlie, Charlie, think of your career." Whether or not Charles thought of his career, the presence of Warren's body between him and his antagonist was enough to distract him, and like a bear thrown off the scent of his enemy, Mingus turned for a few seconds away, while the football player's friends, doubtless also concerned about his career, were able to spirit him out the door before more havoc could occur.

From this I learned that despite his nervousness, despite his frail appearance, Warren was the soul of bravery, ready to take a risk for what he believed in. He believed the art and the soul of Charles Mingus was humanly valuable, and so he was ready to risk his own limbs and safety, as well as his career, to keep that art alive.

It doesn't matter what else anyone might say, there would never have been any poetry of consequence in Vancouver, never any Vancouver poetry scene, without what Warren and Ellen Tallman did. Warren, through Ellen, had a connection to the pulse of living poetry, which at that time in relation to the English language, resided in the United States. Not to say that there was no valuable poetry in Canada. The truth of the matter, contrary to what his detractors said, is that Warren wrote as much about Canadian literature as he did about American literature, even though he never became a Canadian citizen, not because he had contempt for Canadian citizenship, but only because he regarded himself in his naive political way as a citizen of the world.

But every poet is half a fool and every fool is half a poet. The unknown, the un-understood, the unassimilated, the confused and the unfinished are the natural terrain of poetry and the arts, and Warren, as much as anyone, lived within that terrain. The acceptance and recognition of Chaos is one of the most important insights for any contemporary poet. Through Warren, a whole generation of Vancouver poets was privileged to sustain a nourishing relationship with Chaos. From that Chaos has sprung abundant life.

Warren's claim for the substance of his life activities is true: he helped to bring us, the poets of TISH, into the possession of our own imaginations, and there is no greater gift a teacher can give than that.

Symposium: The Line Has Shattered, Simon Fraser University Downtown, August 14, 2009.

NELLIE MCCLUNG
March 21, 1929 – February 13, 2009

Born on the first day of spring in 1929, my dear friend Nellie Lillian McClung died of lung cancer on the evening of February, Friday the13th, 2009 at Mount St. Joseph's Hospital in Vancouver. Nellie was the full-blooded granddaughter of Nellie Letitia McClung, a great Canadian fighter for women's rights and one of the first women ever elected to a Canadian provincial legislature. The elder Nellie was a also a hugely popular writer, speaker and well-known public figure in her own lifetime, and the younger Nellie aspired to follow her grandmother, who designated her as her inheritor.

The younger Nellie was herself the author of at least nine books, mostly of poetry. She said that her ambition was to complete and publish a total of sixteen books in her lifetime, the same number that her grandmother had published.

The features of Nellie's character and personality were very much an echo of her grandmother: a fearless openness, a deep inner innocence, a fabulous courage in following the course of her own vision and destiny.

Her most famous book is a small collection of poems about her idol, Marilyn Monroe, called *My Sex is Ice Cream*, which expressed her own attitudes about sex, love, fame and the place of women in society. Nellie was also a talented amateur painter, whose works have been displayed and sold at various venues in Vancouver. Even in her seventies she often carted her canvasses for long distances on public transit to various galleries, trying to set up shows and sales. She was often rejected, but her spirit of optimism never failed her.

As a young person in Edmonton where she was born, she displayed all of the talents and abilities that might have led to a hugely successful career and wide public acclamation. Tall, and glamourous, she won scholarships to the University of Alberta. She was a star tennis player in her home town, a well-known journalistic personality on the campus of the University of

Alberta, and later on the staff of both the *Edmonton Bulletin* and the *Edmonton Journal*. However, her young life was marked by devastating tragedies. The suicide of her father and the untimely death of her mother left her at the age of twenty in the family home in the Garneau district of Edmonton, to provide income for her younger brother on her own without any knowledge or skills. An early marriage ended in a quick divorce, and thereafter she suffered a series of mental breakdowns.

Throughout much of her adult life, she suffered conspicuously from a mental illness, described in recent psychiatrically fashionable terms as bipolar disorder, previously diagnosed and described variously as schizophrenic, manic-depressive, and various combinations of these two. Although she suffered tremendously from the effects of this disorder throughout her life, she remained a fully intact personality, richer in life, vitality and humanity than many others considered sane and well. In the later stages of her life, new treatments and medications restored her to a basically sound social and mental situation, and throughout her 70s, she was able to carry on her life with huge personal energy—greater than that of many people half her age.

Her life, rich in both tragedy and comedy, opens up on a multitude of important contemporary social themes: mental illness and art; the sexual and social liberation of women; the nature of social and biological inheritance; the social stigma of mental illness; the human rights of the single individual. In particular, the stigma of mental illness, along with a host of other social factors, prevented the younger Nellie from achieving the fame and success that might have accrued to her because of her shining intelligence.

Yet it cannot be said that her life was a human failure—in a certain way it was a greater success than any success of the nominally successful. Her eccentricity points the way to a truth in life transcendently beyond the sanity of those conventionally considered sane.

If the settled and the powerful regarded her dress and

manner, her naïve but talented efforts at art and poetry with contempt and derision, she remained blithely unconcerned. Throughout her life, she had many friends who loved her and delighted in her company. I am proud and privileged to have been one of them.

Here is a poem she wrote to her beloved husband, Peter, whom she insouciantly once described to me: "He used to be gay, but now he's bi-sexual." They loved each other dearly.

Poetry = paper boats "out to sea in the dark." Can't beat that for a metaphor.

SONNET FOR PETER

I hung my poem
about Ireland
out the window
to dry for you
(you lying pale & wan
in your hospital bed)

& soon the gannet & kestrel
small sparrows in twos & threes
alighted at your window
& pecked at the words

& you said it was good
excitement in your voice
"The birdies are here,"
on the phone.

not knowing what to do
with my simple poems
I came each day
and pinned my latest poem
with clothes pins

on a wire across your window
I thought of Chekhov's story we shared
of a man who goes to visit
a hospital patient, & describes
the view out the window, to the enthusiasm
of the patient, the next visitor
saying there was only a brick wall
& again of Li Po who put his poems
in lighted candled paper boats
and sent them out to sea in the dark.

And here's another paper boat sent into the dark, from me, to Nellie.

NELLIE MCCLUNG

Saw the Jesus and the Buddha
with her own two blue eyes in Ottawa.

The Buddha was on land,
came through the wall, in fact,
as she was meditating.

And later that same evening,
she saw Jesus
as she floated on the river
like Ophelia.

The passengers who passed her
on board the pleasure cruiser
must have seen her:
just another piece of smooth white ice
drifting on that winter river.

Nellie's white raincoat
bouyed her up and saved her life.
If she'd been wearing black,
those river fishermen
who took the name of Christ in vain &
saved her life
would've never seen her.

After seeing Buddha,
she didn't think
that she could sink.
She's the only one
I've ever known personally
who ever saw them both
on the selfsame evening.

That's two for you, Nellie.
Never occurred to you until later,
that you might not be worthy.

That's why I stay away
from anything religious nowadays,
Nellie says,
I get carried away, you know.

The poem "Sonnet for Peter" is from the chapbook, *Charles Tupper & Me*, Coracle Press © Nellie McClung, 2004, 2012.

The Poem "Nelly McClung" was published in *I Another: The Space Between*, by Jamie Reid, Talonbooks, 2004.

NEIL EUSTACHE, ENFANT TERRIBLE

I missed the last eclipse[1] is the title of a new chapbook from a new Vancouver publishing house called Panarky Press in collaboration with Hugo Fly Publishing. Its author, Neil Eustache, is a twenty-six year old street poet living in Vancouver. To call Eustache a "street poet" is to put a limitation on the universal message of his work. And although he comes from a Native background, to call him a Native poet is also to impose arbitrary limits on his work that he himself rejects, although it may help to locate part of his cultural sources.

His work, like all real poetry, both reflects and transcends the conditions of its production. Eustache is a representative of the fag-end of the modernist tradition of poetry, the tradition which has roots with the *déclassé* Francois Villon in the 14th Century and begins its modern incarnation with Baudelaire and Rimbaud in the last half of the nineteenth century, runs through the poets Blaise Cendrars, Guillaume Appolinaire, and Antonin Artaud, appears again in the post-war work of such diverse writers as Albert Camus, Jean Genet, Raymond Chandler, Allen Ginsberg and Jack Kerouac and has been iconicized in the movie figures of James Dean, Marlon Brando and Jean-Paul Belmondo.

Even if Eustache has not been directly influenced by these literary and cultural figures, the social atmosphere from which his writing comes is the same. He is a poete maudit manqué — in spite of himself. His writing is the poetry of the "bad boy," the *enfant terrible*, the unrepentant punk.

The spite and resigned anger which his poetry delivers as often as not is directed against himself as much as against the world. His main themes are hate and violence, which he despises, yet accepts as possibly permanent features of the human world. All his tales are those of unhappy beginnings and unhappy endings. Yet the aura of the apocalypse is entirely missing in this poetry, for this is a country where the world ends not with a bang but a whimper.

The poetry in this genre (for by now, it has become a genre) is an urban poetry founded on the ennui, disillusion, alienation and spiritual emptiness of the modern city dweller, forcibly divorced from the healing power of nature, at odds with all established authority and belief, bereft of all spiritual comfort. The prevailing mood of this poetry is a kind of glory in decay, a memory of the ardent and false dreams of the past, an ironic contempt for deceitful images of the future. It is the intellectual property of the deprived, the tradition of those without tradition. Intellectually, this poetry stems from the nihilism of the nineteenth century, from Neitzsche, and by now, it has traversed all the terrain beyond good and evil, beyond hope and despair, beyond love and hate.

There are no supermen, no *Übermenschen* in this world, where the life of human beings is reduced to the level of insects and vermin:

"First we go to the park to drink and take a piss, and drink some more / We are drunk, so drunk that the park is now the street, and the street is / full of rats, just like my buddy, busy rats running, in the cage of a city, a / hell of a city"

This is the poetry of the human being deprived of any useful social role—the criminal, the loser, the outcast, the permanent outsider without a way to get back in, who has apparently lost even the desire to get back in, and so clings to a kind of fierce pride in the status of outcast, as though it were a personal choice, rather than a socially-dictated necessity.

This is the poetry of the human being deprived of community except in the most blind and primitive sense, the sense in which human relations are reduced to the exchange of commodities—cigarettes, alcohol, sex—bought and paid for. Whether Eustache draws his knowledge from the intellectual and literary tradition of the recent past, or whether he arrives at his conclusions through his own mental activities, the truth remains the same—the human conditions for the production of these outpourings of negativism continue to exist as part of the fabric of the social reality of capitalist society. As much as the social organism continues to produce wealth at one end of its spectrum, it continues to generate poverty and despair at the other. You want to explain the hatred and violence that tortures the world? Look to the gulf between the haves and the have-nots, between the rich and the poor.

The poetry of Neil Eustache operates under the sign of a NO, which declares itself without any real hope of the existence of a contradictory YES, of another and more humane order of things, which might possibly cancel the negativity that he sees. The metaphysics of negation has its correspondence in the aesthetics of ugliness. It does not dress itself up. It walks naked and bald. It strives neither to convince nor to seduce—only to offend and repel. It makes no direct appeals or demands. For Eustache, poetry is an offensive act committed against an offensive world. On the other hand, it makes no excuses, either. It merely records a profound absence, the absence of humanity. In its active forms, it exists on the verge of rape and murder:

"You have your way, I have mine
You have your gun and I have mine
You and I will kill, you and I will lie, you and I will be alive"

"...I had a nerve that was / bothering me, a nerve that had a killer behind it, ready to be let out. I / had the nerve."

In its passive forms, it exists on the verge of suicide and self-annihilation:

"I turn to my typewriter for reality, for guidance, for control / I turn on my mind to masturbate my soul, to jack off my heart, to beat my / dreams senseless / I smoke and live like a man that knows nothing of the future / the future knows me better than I know myself."

In these poems, the process of living, more often than not, is signified by the acts of smoking, drinking, sitting in a chair, watching television, defecating, writing. Each of these represents a form of relief, a turning away, a means of eliminating pain and the consciousness of pain. Cigarettes, television, the passing cars—all of the instruments and symbols of the capitalist consumer society which consume human flesh and consciousness just as they present themselves to be consumed and are consumed.

All this being said, Neil Eustache in person, as distinct from in performance or on the page, is a harmless and amiable human being whose talk is made up of comical, though often horrendous accounts of his experience in life, the violence of his relatives and associates. He is himself the victim of violence rather than the author of it, and is fully aware of the senselessness of violence and hatred. His typical pose is of the mild, passive observer, full of resigned amusement at the folly of other human beings.

When the entire body of his work is viewed as one piece rather than in the narrative fragments in which it is first given and first appears to the reader's consciousness, a consistent poetic voice is heard to raise itself above the circumstances which this same voice chronicles. With a kind of shock, we realize that it is not just the world of Eustache and the world of the down-and-outer that is being represented, but the very same world in which we, too, live in the absence of any real humanity or human concern.

Just at the moment when the reader is prepared to reject Eustache's discourse as pure simple-mindedness, the lyric element within his work makes itself sharply felt, only to disappear again into the blighted pond of his indifference. Yet at bottom, this is a style, a mask, a pose. Beneath the mask we find a highly aware and conscious individual. Where the lyric adornments appear, they signal a vision of the anti-human horrors of the modern world. Yes, it is a one-sided vision, but its truth and effectiveness depend precisely on this same one-sidedness.

Those who are tempted to complain that Eustache reflects

only the horrors and not the glories of modern technological civilization need to remember that Eustache and "his kind" do not receive any of the benefits of this so-called civilization. Eustache seems to have accepted this condition in good and even happy conscience, rejecting the benefits as well as the absence, understanding that the two of them are part and parcel of the same reality, and that one side of the equation cannot logically be rejected without also rejecting the other, and if anything, Eustache is conscious of this logic.

What new reality can emerge from such a consciousness? Eustache himself does not seem to know, even though there is a sadness in his work that signals a desire for something else. One thing is definite: Eustache cannot sustain his career as a poet by remaining where he is. Some new element must come into his work if he is to avoid creative suicide. Improved craft alone will not solve the contradiction. If Eustache confines his efforts merely to improving his craft alone, nothing valuable can ensue, and it is hard to imagine how, from this profound sense of absence, he will be able to continue to generate a sense of presence.

Yet things have a way of turning into their opposites. When the crisis of negativism reaches its sharpest point, the result is either death or a new form of life. And the poetic career of Neil Eustache is headed sharply toward that crisis.

---

1. *I Missed the Last Eclipse*, Neil Eustache, 1994, Hugo Fly Pub./Panarky Press.

ONLY THE GOOD DIE YOUNG

"i am here to learn and to absorb and reflect and to be reflected..."[1]

Poetry circles in Vancouver today are grieving the loss of T.Paul Ste. Marie, self-described "low brow spoken word artist," but also a major promoter and impresario of the art of the spoken word, as it is called these days, in order to distinguish this poetry of the streets from the poetry of universities, books and libraries. T.Paul sadly died last Thursday at the untimely age of 41, following a disabling brain aneurism that felled him terribly a year ago, and from which apparently he never fully recovered. T.Paul will be remembered above all as the founder, organizer and indefatigable emcee, host and performer of the Thundering Word Heard at the Montmartre Café, one of Vancouver's longest living and most popular spoken word performance venues.

The Vancouver poetry scene was never the same after T.Paul's arrival from points east several years ago. The absence of his unrelenting activity and energy occasioned by his aneurism last year has already left a hole that can't and won't be filled by anyone else, because T.Paul was a unique and inimitable personality. The echo and shadow of his legacy will surely survive at least a little while in the deep undercurrents of the city, but no shadow can be securely sanforized, no image permanently inscribed in the world of rapidly changing, interchangeable images of today's consumer culture, dominated by television and its advertising. And the dominating feature of T.Paul's activity was its deliberate ephemerality and impermanence. It was essentially performance art, whose effect on the world at large is always the result of a momentary spark lit between the performer and a live audience. A once-only kind of thing, its only permanent essence is its momentariness, its ephemerality, unlike the words that last apparently forever on the pages of books.

T.Paul deeply understood what many others apparently don't, that the hidden corners and interstices of the vulgar world of popular myth and legend, of shady representation and misrepresentation, contain a necessary cosmic joke on the solemnities of history and contemporary social life. T-Paul happily and quite earnestly lived out his own cosmic joke, a life of fantasy on the fringes of polite society and art, inviting others in droves to join with him, which they merrily did.

T.Paul uniquely brought what are too often disparagingly labelled as the arts of intrigue, publicity and "shameless self-promotion" as he called it, to the promotion of his own verbal art and that of many others in his broad community. With deliberate irony and self-irony, T.Paul linked cheesy showbiz with poetry, in some eyes a crime, in other eyes, a welcome and a necessary play.

Out of the generosity of his activity, T.Paul created and lighted a space for numerous other performance poets and artists besides himself. He was slighted and sometimes derided for this in some literary circles as much as he was loved and praised in others. Throughout his life, he never became nationally or even locally famous other than in his own self-chosen demi-world, his own community of like-minded friends. He remained throughout his life a fringe denizen, an under-grounder by inclination and by nature, a dweller in the fascinating and sometimes bizarre back channels of modern popular culture, but particularly of the counterculture, that realm of resistance to the established order that begins with the image of the rebel rockabilly punk, because that was the image that T.Paul chose for himself above all other possible memes he might have chosen.

His work in poetry and performance was popular and vulgar rather than exalted and exclusive, more humorous than profound. He himself would have been the last to proclaim his life and work in any way resembled anything refined and exalted, and much less anything resembling a permanent "high, fine art." He scrambled among his contemporaries and his community of friends for light and presence in the living city of the present, and made no pretense to immortality or holiness for his art. He was a spiritual rather than a religious person, probably preferring small household gods to any other kind of god. There were many small shrines in his house dedicated to different small deities he professed a fondness for.

He was a busy and an active person, an entrepreneurial soul, an unassuming and unpretentious professional in everything he did, though he never made or even seemed to aspire toward anything more than a bare living from his many activities. In that sense, his art was always an activity carried out for others as much as for himself. His many activities, according to his own resume, included "emcee/host, singer, dancer (some — jazz, modern, ballroom), character voices — dialects & accents, kung fu, specialized martial arts & weapons handling, western horseback riding, mime, clowning, fire breathing, billiards, C.P.R./A.R./first aid, writer of scripts, short stories and poetry, painter/fine artist, graphic & computer graphic design, promoter, producer of live events."

In the self-reflective process of unraveling some of the threads of his varied identity, T.Paul himself proclaimed: "I have some difficulty with the lines between who I am and what I do as they're so intertwined, so if this profile comes across as a messy mélange of 'Hello—this is me!' and shameless self-promotion, it's only 'cause the lines are so bloody blurred in my own view." (from people.tribe)

From the top of his Brylcreem pompadour to his billowy strides, his wingtip shoes and his argyle socks, he was, within his self-created self, the repository and the mirror of most of the trends in what's rightly or wrongly been called popular or mass culture since World War II and earlier. An unerring instinct guided him to what was best and most iconic in that culture, the funkily romantic, the spots where meaning and terror meet, along with its typical lighthearted humour and frivolity. His self-made identity was not so much an integrated stream as a playful patchwork collage, incorporating elements nostalgically and sentimentally from different iconic sources. His various websites feature photos of his heroes, who include Bob Fosse, the beat poet Ted Joans, and Tom Waits, but also Marlon Brando and James Dean. Among his many collected items of trailer park art, he claims that one of his most prized possessions is a set of drumsticks given to him by the all-time great jazz drummer, Buddy Rich.

His self-designation was "swankhipster."

The happy angels laugh; the solemn devils groan.

T.Paul the person and the personality was a sincere class act. He had a good and generous heart and did what he did for others more than for himself. I'm glad he was in the city for all kinds of reasons, and I am very sorry he's now gone.

In the culture of celebrity, most of the celebrities are freaked up commodities disguised as real people. T.Paul, in his earnest *détournement* of popular culture, was a real person freaked up as a commodity.

---

1. From: T. Paul's Profile on <<tribe.net>>

KIM GOLDBERG'S RED ZONE: URBAN PLASTIC SURGERY

"In December 2007, upon decree of a provincial court Judge, Nanaimo's Red Zone was expanded by several orders of magnitude. It is now bounded by Fitzwilliam and Bastion Streets on the north, and by Milton and Esplanade on the south. This is nearly forty blocks. Basically all of downtown Nanaimo. Previously it had been one block. To be banned from the Red Zone, one need not be tried and convicted of a crime but merely accused of one."

Kim Goldberg baldly declares her poetic intent in the pages of *Red Zone*, her utterly remarkable self-published multi-media work about homelessness in Canada's Vancouver Island city of Nanaimo.

> *...I'm an urban*
> *plastic surgeon remodelling the skin of this*
> *declining milltown swelled with mallbloat Let's make it pop*
> *and sing and splay the rat-torn epic of*
> *late capitalism in fluorescent orange This is the language*
> *of rejoinder in a grilled cheese world encased*
> *in its own sloppy grease The language of things*
> *that cannot be said Of things*
> *that cannot be permitted to be true The language of*
> *unerasure (no matter how many times*
> *It is obliterated) The language*
> *of being*
> *of existence*
> *of We Are Here*

The outstanding feature of *Red Zone* as poetry is its manifest intent to exert immediate influence on the daily world in Nanaimo, the particular city and place from which it comes. The book has been completely fashioned as an item of practical use, a living document and instrument, a kind of lever in the hands of its readers for moving minds and hearts, actively shaking easy complacencies, arousing consciousness and conscience, and thereby laying conditions for bringing changes to the social environment, even if the civic authorities of Nanaimo continue to remain deaf and blind to their citizens.

The Red Zone decree bans the homeless of Nanaimo from access to the very services they require in the city's core: the needle exchange, health care and the food bank. Goldberg's book provides a flesh-rending vision of the harsh life these people are forced to lead. More importantly, it provides a life-saving and self-affirming vision to those she writes about. In this sense, the book is a kind of survival manual for living in the urban hell created by the indifferent cruelty of Nanaimo's civic authorities.

As a self-declared "plastic surgeon" of the real, Goldberg's aim is not to create an artificial "poetic" beauty, but rather to surgically remove the masks that hide the ugliness of poverty and homelessness that have become a reality in every urban landscape, not only in Nanaimo, but throughout the world of late capitalism where huge wealth exists alongside such abject poverty and want.

Although it is pre-eminently a collection of poems, *Red Zone* is a truly genre-busting work in the best postmodern style, combining pop-art features with sophisticated language practice. Liberally interspersed with her poems, the included photographs and graphics showcase graffiti slogans and drawings in the Nanaimo cityscape — the decidedly unpicturesque objects and vistas of poverty and urban decay. The images found in the book are at once found art objects and documentary signs, sharp and funny comments on the crimes and absurdities of a brutal social order where social problems are erased and disguised and hidden away, rather than solved.

Goldberg is an activist, and she energetically puts her body where her mouth is, carries her book out into the streets, making it available in as many places as she can, reading poems wherever she can, from universities to urban underpasses where the homeless actually live and sleep. For Goldberg, a book exists manifestly not as a dead object on a library shelf, but as part of her own life practice, part of her own life activity of engaging people and the world.

> *I want to learn if utterance can change the thing being spoken about. Will these mastodon columns [of the underpasses where the homeless sleep] release their hallowed souls?*
>
> *One never knows these things if poetry won't leave the haven of the coffeehouse, won't stand on the precipice, wind-smacked, tongue-kissing the infinite.*

The genuineness of her concern has been rewarded, as few poets these days are, by a living audience beyond the narrow circles of university writers and the CanLit literati: her book went into a second printing three months after it appeared, and it has already been included on the syllabus of several Vancouver Island university courses.

But *Red Zone* is much more than a didactic social diatribe. Beneath its pop and comic-book-like exterior, this book also succeeds as poetry because it combines all of its essential elements: passion, intensity, an engagement with the intricacies of language and linguistic forms, startling imagery, subtle and challenging ideas, a rough but magical music, and a happily antic inventive spirit.

It's impossible to provide a full account of the manifold modest treasures the book contains, including its many inventive uses of old forms. A sequence of 11 haikus brings fresh and telling images to a form usually more pastoral than urban:

> *small dog in plaid coat*
>   *trots past sleeping bag, leaves frosty*
>   *stitch of paw prints*
>
> *fourth week of snow*
>   *and only the unitarians open*
>   *their doors*

A series of mimotypes, described by Goldberg as "a form that resembles another in general shape but not genetic make-up," balances pastoral images against urban images to create a series of sharp contrasts that combine to make an environmental as well as a semantic statement about the shifting meanings of words:

> *Crumpled as the bracken unfurling each spring*
> *Crumpled as the beer cans hurled from diesel stinking cabs*
>
> *Flat as the red wing blackbird's black eye*
> *Flat as the real estate sign that went up last night*

She ends with a plea both ambiguous and challenging in its hopeful humanism:

> *We are more than subject-verb-predicate*
> *We are more than a governing device*
> *We are more than war bled dry, epicenter aslaughter*
> *We are more than warbled dry epic, enter as laughter*
> *We are more*

It would be nice to say that the world needs more poetry like that of *Red Zone*, but like any worthwhile work of poetry or art, Kim Goldberg's work is quite truly one of a kind.

RED ZONE: *Poems of Homelessness & Urban Decay*, Kim Goldberg, 2009, Pig Squash Press.

IGNITING THE GREEN FUSE: FOUR CANADIAN WOMEN POETS

Eco-poetry is at once aesthetic and political, because it counterposes the beauty and power of the natural environment against the depredations and destructions of nature caused by human industrialized societies.

Its aim is to nurture feelings and attitudes that enhance and encourage the political action required to rescue the planet and all of its biological life from impending wreckage and burnout caused by human economic action.

Eco-poetry therefore integrates climate science, biology, nomenclature of lost and threatened species, political commentary, and many other factors to bring together an all-sided vision of the interface between the natural non-human and the human mechanical/industrial, which threatens to overwhelm the planet.

Often enough, eco-poetry enacts an apocalyptical drama of the imminent or on-going industrial destruction of the natural biosphere against the background of a nostalgic pastoral narrative.

"...there is no universally accepted definition of 'eco-poetry,'" Kim Goldberg writes in her introduction to this new chapbook. In the interests of "showing rather than telling," the four female poets contributing to the collection decided to "...show you what each of us considers eco-poetic in our own practice."

The result of their collaboration is a small and attractive showcase displaying the widely different poetic styles and sensibilities of four British Columbian female poets, each with a different approach to their common environmental theme.

As a book which features poems by women only, *Igniting the Green Fuse* seems equally to suggest a second, feminist, political dimension alongside its environmental message. If the green fuse that metaphorically sets off explosive nature in the Dylan

Thomas poem can be ignited by human agency, is this task in some way especially the provenance of women? The question remains implicit rather than being explicitly answered here. Yet implicitly the fact that women are speaking to this issue and are speaking together, contains its own meaning in relation to the past and the future of the environmental movement.

The work of Kim Goldberg typically spans the gap between literary activity and social act. As the first poet in the book, she launches her patented rush of vital energy, a flash of explosive imagery in which words that traditionally act as signifiers of poetry and lyrical pastorality are ironically undercut by descriptions of the mangling of living things by destructive industrial power:

The salty air packed tight today with sirens' wail
in Japanese markets, while the yawning emptiness of our elections
echoes in the darkened hold to be later stripped and sold
as fish bait. We watched the morning stars cascade into
a diesel-flowered meadow binding all our heads, beating
while it burned until the stench and smoky spew
was traded for the flickerflash of atomic churn.
(Spawn)

Bravely breaking gender barriers, Kate Braid for fifteen years earned her living as a professional carpenter, from which experience she embraced a practical attitude toward wood. Lumber is made from natural trees, and Braid discovers and uncovers something sacred not only in the natural wood itself, but in the productive relationship between herself, a human maker, and her natural materials:

... your spirit stares
and sees what is between the trees
joining them.
A space
any carpenter would understand.

It is the reason that we build things.
Looks like air to some,
fresh breeze, a touch of chill
or fog.
It is the spirit of the tree.

Now I know who you are.
Another woman who loves wood.
   (Wood Interior)

A common ground in the love of nature and its beauties belongs to all these poets. Catherine Owen is a modernist poet with a romantic-gothic-dramatic bent, perhaps best expressed by the fact that she chooses the crow as her totem animal. Most recently, she writes as a river dweller from an apartment above the Fraser River in south Vancouver, thriving on the juxtapositions between destructive human activity and the irrepressible drive of animal and vegetable life to flourish and continuously grow in the face of every effort of human civilization to contain and bury it:

Thick winch of ripped rope at the base of a rusted bolt,
Beside it, a skimpy alder sapling,
all sprouting from a relic of fallen log, saw marks chunked with dirt

& clover. These the juxtapositions I live for....
   (Fraser River, Thanksgiving 2011)

I especially like the apparently casual and colloquial asides in Owen's poems, where the full meanings suddenly appear in an apparently offhand way:

– why not keep
Just the tiny breathing apparatus – the crows do – tumbling from
the parapets –

*Black chutes sagging open – go river! Go river! – I'm cheering mostly
For the water now – loving how it's always moving past me.*
  (I feel the tree's grief – why can't I say this)

Heidi Greco envisions a world where industrial/consumer society and culture tames and overwhelms nature with its organization and civilization and defiles it with its detritus and its bland containing order:

*The shortcuts and byways have all been replaced
by squared off yards smoothed flat with lawns, trimmed
in conventional styles – just so many haircuts in a row.
Everyone lies awake at night, aligned in their king-size beds,
clutching remotes instead of each other, warmed
by the flickering light that shines like a squared off moon in the night,
And all the while the people keep dreaming, tired but open-eyed,
trying to think up one more gadget to buy.*
  (The Dreams We Take For Silence)

This world of consumer detritus, cigarette butts, paper coffee cups and empty bottles swept up in alleys by gleaners in the dark, also ends with a mock apocalypse:

*5 leggy dandelions, golden
of throat, leaning back, set to play
some final trumpet blast.*
  (Walking Inventory, November)

This book intends to help provoke something more prosaic—political activity to bring social change on the environmental front. It's deliberately a small and modest production, a simple chapbook, and only a single drop in the huge bucket of activity required for the solution of this most pressing issue facing all of humanity and its world. But every drop can be made to count. Readers who are already fans of these four poets, as I am, will enjoy its content and style, and for those who aren't already fans, this chapbook is an excellent place to start the process of coming to know their work.

"Igniting the Green Fuse: Four Canadian Women Poets" was originally published May 24, 2012 on Jamie's blog: Schroedinger's Cat (http://canitplease.blogspot.ca) as "Four Canadian Women Poets Eco Poetry, Kim Goldberg's Red Zone."

Acknowledgements

I wish to thank Brian Kaufman, publisher of Anvil Press, and editor Karl Siegler, for rescuing this manuscript and bringing it to the light of day.

Thanks also go to my sister, Eve Joseph, who scoured the manuscript for a clue to the book's title, and found it; and to Lary Bremner for his assistance with a myriad of questions surrounding the true meaning of Fake Poems.

To the community of poets and friends who have believed in this project and supported it with such generosity, thank you.

And to Jamie, who once said, "One day I hope to write a poem or book that will hold everyone's attention and perhaps redeem my life on earth," my love and gratitude for this your last, beautiful book.

—Carol Reid, November, 2016

ABOUT THE AUTHOR

Jamie Reid (April 10, 1941 – June 25, 2015) was a Canadian writer, activist, and arts organizer. He was born in Timmins, Ontario and came of age on the west coast of Canada.

Reid was one of the founding editors of the influential poetry journal TISH in Vancouver in 1961 with George Bowering, Frank Davey, David Dawson, and Fred Wah. He published his first collection of poems, *The Man Whose Path Was on Fire*, in 1969. A short time later he joined the Communist Party of Canada (Marxist-Leninist) and stopped writing for twenty-five years in favour of political activism "because [he] didn't have a way of working the language of politics into the language of poetry."[1]

Reid returned to poetry and cultural criticism in the late 1980s, with a special interest in jazz expressed in many of his works. He lived in North Vancouver with his wife, the painter Carol Reid, since returning to Vancouver in 1990, and their home was a hub of literary activism and activity, including the publication of his local/international avant-garde magazine *DaDaBaBy*. Reid also edited and contributed to the intergenerational Vancouver literary journal *Tads* (1996-2001) through which Reid, George Bowering, Renee Rodin, and George Stanley mentored younger writers, including Thea Bowering, Wayde Compton, Reg Johanson, Ryan Knighton, Jason le Heup, Cath Morris, Chris Turnbull, and Karina Vernon.

Jamie Reid was a member of the original five-member editorial board of TISH, the Vancouver poetry newsletter at UBC, in 1961. He became a co-organizer (with many others), and a spokesperson for, the first Vancouver Human Be-In in Stanley Park, in 1967.

Jamie Reid's formative experiences with TISH at UBC led him to be influenced by local writers such as George Bowering, Frank Davey, Fred Wah, Gladys Hindmarch and Lionel Kearns. In turn, he came to know and respect other

Vancouver poets that included John Newlove, Gerry Gilbert, bill bissett, Peter Trower, Barry McKinnon, Maxine Gadd, Judith Copithorne and many others. Poets who came to Vancouver and influenced him have included Robert Duncan, Robert Creeley, Jack Spicer, Al Purdy, Milton Acorn and Louis Dudek. "All of these poets gave something to me," he says, "showed me something about life and about poetry."

Jamie Reid died at home on June 25, 2015.

---

1. We would like to acknowledge the Wikipedia entry "Jamie Reid (Canadian Poet)" and ABCBookworld as sources for biographical information on Jamie Reid.